The Prince Charles Letters

The Prince Charles Letters

Compiled by David Stubbs

Aurum

First published 2011 by
Aurum Press Limited
7 Greenland Street
London NW1 0ND
www.aurumpress.co.uk

A catalogue record for this book is available from the British Library.

ISBN 978 1 84513 681 9
Ebook ISBN 978 1 84513 737 3

10 9 8 7 6 5 4 3 2 1
2015 2014 2013 2012 2011

Typeset by MRules

Printed and bound in Great Britain by
MPG Books, Bodmin, Cornwall

To Alisha – my little Princess

Contents

Introduction

In recent months it has emerged that Prince Charles has long been in the habit of writing highly opinionated letters to various government ministries and departments. This revelation has provoked anxious debate as to whether the Prince is exceeding himself in attempting to influence policy in this way. Is he overstepping his constitutional bounds, or quite properly and democratically airing his views as Prince of the realm and concerned citizen?

Certainly, there have been calls for the letters to be made public in order that their contents can be laid open to wider scrutiny. And now, thanks to one of the most extraordinary leaks of modern times, we can see, for the first time, the full extent of the Prince's tireless epistolary efforts.

It was approaching 5.45 in the evening, just as staff were leaving for the day, when a stooped, haggard fellow with the elegant but harassed air of a gentleman's personal gentleman appeared, unannounced in the office doorway at Aurum's publishing HQ. Reception hadn't buzzed him up — it later turned out that he'd slipped in via an open window in the back alleyway. Half-hiding his face in his lapels, he scuttled up to reception, deposited a jiffy bag on the desk, mumbling something about a 'package from his employer', then scuttled off, out the doorway and down the stairs with the alacrity of a cockroach. An Aurum editor gingerly approached the package, which, it turned out, contained a memory stick. On that memory stick were discovered scanned-in copies of hundreds of letters sent by Prince Charles, spanning seven decades. The decks were immediately cleared at Aurum — all staff were tasked with poring over this remarkable cache of material.

Even at first glance, it was clear that this was a veritable trove. What was most remarkable was the sheer breadth of Charles's addressees. Up until now, he was thought to have confined himself to writing to government. As well as Presidents, Prime Ministers and his Holiness the Pope, we now see that he has long considered it his business to write to a whole range of public figures from the worlds of sport, popular music, the arts and show business. From Tracy Emin to Sir Alex Ferguson. From Fiona Bruce to Michael McIntyre. From Lady Gaga and Justin Bieber to Harold Pinter and Charlie Sheen. He has taken the trouble, as future King, to establish a rapport with these famous individuals, express his admiration, give career advice where appropriate, attempt to involve them in his own good works (Outward Bound, the Prince's Trust) or simply to ask them who, exactly, they are.

There are recurring correspondences. He has a jovial, backslapping rapport with former Deputy Prime Minister John Prescott, for example, to whom he writes frequently, although sadly we are not privy to Mr Prescott's responses, if any, to the Prince's thoughts and suggestions. His Highness also corresponds with regularity to Eileen Derbyshire, better known as *Coronation Street*'s Emily Bishop, whom he appears to regard as a mother figure, of the sort he perhaps lacked in his formative years.

We see Charles at his best tussling with the great minds of

the day, including Jean-Paul Sartre on the topic of
existentialism. As he patiently explains to the Frenchman, it's
not just about 'being', it's about 'doing' – getting things
done – the Charles philosophy, arguably the superior one, in a
nutshell. He also upbraids Sir John Betjeman and Ted Hughes
when he suspects that their hearts are not always in the verses
they submit when called upon to commemorate important
Royal occasions.

For Charles, correspondence is a means of expressing his
most profound speculations about life, the Universe, the self,
the soul. Hence letters addressed to Mankind, to the leader of
any party of aliens to have established first contact with planet
earth, to God and to the plant kingdom, with whom Charles
has long pressed for a meaningful dialogue.

A picture emerges, too, of Charles's family, through
illustrative anecdotes peppered throughout the
correspondence and in letters to the likes of HRH Princess
Anne, the late Queen Mother, Prince Philip and the Queen
herself. At times we sense a certain distance in these
relationships and yet they prove revealing of precisely the level
of esteem in which Charles is held by other Royals, even if that
level is not always high.

Charles is also a man of paradoxes; one who believes that
in order to go forwards we must go backwards, and that while
there are many alternatives there is, in the case of the
Monarchy, for example, no alternative. Charles is a man who
is very, very concerned. About everyone and everything. And
that concern invariably hovers around the level of tremendous,
often hitting the heights of 'extremely'. He at once avoids
dogmatic, precise prescriptions and the woolly, bureaucratic
rhetoric of inaction. Something, he says, firmly, time and
again, must be done. What that entails is a detail he leaves to
smaller men – technicians, functionaries and so forth.

There cannot be discounted the possibility that the letters

are not in fact, genuine; an elaborate literary hoax. Certainly, some of Charles's correspondents appear to be under the impression they are counterfeit, to the Prince's occasional exasperation, as it means his letters too frequently end up going ignored altogether.

Surely, however, a hoaxer, motivated by malice and mischief, would not go to so much trouble to create the flattering and impressive picture that emerges of the Prince from these correspondences — a man constantly striving to get past the material distractions of modern life, back to the soil and to the soul, back to a golden age where balance and harmony were reconciled. A man not afraid to use what he calls the 'non-intellectual realm' of the mind, as inspired by his mentor Laurens Van Der Post. A man who at once strives to be an 'ordinary chap', as much a fan of Status Quo as the next, yet who deep in his heart realises that the role for which he is constantly grasping is potentially a huge one, embracing all faiths, all species, and which straddles both the material and non-material worlds.

We must accept, then, on balance, that these are the definite article — but who was responsible for the leak of these letters, some written in Charles's childhood, others composed only a few months ago? It seems hard to believe that it was any member of his staff, who at all times show themselves to be one hundred per cent amenable to absolutely every thought and idea expressed by their employer. This surely cannot be because they know, to coin a phrase 'which side their bread is buttered' but is more likely out of genuine inspiration at his Vision.

Perhaps a clue lies in the note which accompanied the memory stick, only discovered days later, having dropped from the jiffy bag and become attached to the bottom of a chair leg. It is anonymous; it reads as follows:

To whom this may concern

Look here, one can't tell you how one got hold of these letters but, you know, I really think it would be appalling if they never saw the light of day. One has sweated over them — that is to say, Charles, sweated over them — and hang it all, some of us believe he's a jolly misunderstood 'fellow', who ought to have been King a jolly sight sooner than he's going to be, while Mama — his Mama, our Queen — continues to be so bally 'stubborn'. Do you what you will with these, there's good fellows. You'd be obliging your future Sovereign, who knows nothing about all of this, but would definitely, absolutely approve. These letters show the real Charles — unlike myself, who is not the real Charles, I must make that clear. Nor is it either of my brothers, or my sister for that matter.

Yours, &c
Mr X

We may never know the true identity of 'Mr X'. However, we are eternally in his debt for providing us with a quite extraordinary glimpse into the mental workings of our future King.

David Stubbs
July 2011

Leaders of Britain
(For a Short While)

Harold Macmillan
10 Downing Street
London
England   21 November 1958

Dear Mr Macmillan

I've been thinking a lot about politics and I've decided that I'm
a supporter of the Labour Party. I know you're for the
Conservatives, but that's all right — it's just that I'm for Labour.

I think everyone should have absolutely equal shares. At the
end of every month, they should count up just how much money
the country has made that month, then take the number of
grown-up people in the country and give each of them exactly
the same amount. They could send them the money by postal
orders with those whose names begin with 'A' to 'D' getting
theirs on a Monday, 'E' to 'G' getting theirs on a Tuesday, and
so on to stop there being queues at the Post Offices.

Of course, the Royal Family would have to get extra because
we've got special duties and things we need to look after, like
the Crown, the Throne and all the dogs, but I think it would
work jolly well for everyone else. Oh, and everyone should wear
top hats, not just the posh people . . . and they should be
MADE to wear them, even if they don't want to, because that's
being equal.

> Yours, in equality
> Master Windsor (Charles)

Harold Macmillan
10 Downing Street
London
England   13 October 1961

Dear Mr Macmillan

In our Geography class we had to read up today about the
population explosion. Our teacher says we are making too many
babies. If there's a population explosion, I don't mind sharing my
room with Andrew but I'm NOT sharing with Anne because she's
a girl and she'll just clutter everything up with her dolls and horse
things. But then she would get to have a room to herself, which
isn't fair because I'm sharing with Andrew. So we should agree that
if Mummy makes another baby, then Anne should have to share
her room with the new baby, who might be a boy or a girl. Would
you share your room with the Chancellor of the Exchequer?

        Yours truly
        Charles

Harold Wilson
10 Downing Street
London
England   17 October 1964

Dear Mr Wilson

Speaking as a prince and a mature schoolboy looking forward to
being a grown-up of the future, I am writing to congratulate
you on becoming Prime Minister and wish you well in forming
my mother's Government.

I was very excited by that speech you made about the 'white heat of technology'. Last Christmas, I was given a Meccano set by my Uncle Dickie and it's provided me with heaps of fun. I expect by the year 2000 pretty much everything in the whole world will be made out of Meccano, which is quite thrilling in some ways but also a bit of a worry. Will it all stay up? Mine often doesn't. I don't think I have a future in architecture!

Well, must dash – I have a short meeting with Father. By the way, you've met Ringo Starr. Could you ask him why he hasn't replied to the letter I sent him?

> Futuristically, yours
> Charles

Edward Heath
10 Downing Street
London
England   20 June 1970

Dear Mr Heath

On behalf of myself and my sister and two brothers, I'd like to take this opportunity to congratulate you as you 'set sail' on your leadership of a new Conservative Government. I must say, I'm inclined to think British politics is a bit like a 'see-saw', with Labour on one side and the Conservatives on the other, and it would be interesting to see how the Liberals fared if they were given a chance under Mr Thorpe. I think that's what the vast majority of sensible people would like to see, although they never seem to vote for it, which is rather queer. But you're in charge now, so I suppose we all just have to hope you do a good job.

I like your ideas about Conservatism with a human face. I've always felt the best sort of Conservative is a smiling one and I've met a few over the years. Winston Churchill was sometimes a bit gruff, like a bulldog on an enforced vegetarian diet. Mr Macmillan was OK, though I didn't like it when he said that we'd 'never had it so good' – I was at Gordonstoun at the time. Not a cheering thought when you've spent the afternoon being mock crucified with tent pegs on a bicycle-shed door! Anthony Eden always looked rather ill. In fact, all the Conservative Prime Ministers I met became very ill during their time in charge. You're feeling quite well, I hope?

Anyway, congratulations again to you and Mrs Heath.

> Yours faithfully
> Charles, POW (Prince of Wales, not the other kind!)

Jim Callaghan
10 Downing Street
London
England   6 April 1976

Dear Mr Callaghan

I expect you're as surprised as everyone else was to find yourself Prime Minister after all these years, but as my father is fond of saying, 'Wonders never bloody cease!' A bit salty, I know, but not too shocking for a man of your naval background, I'm sure.

I don't envy you, I must say – scowling punk rockers, litter in the streets, faceless tower blocks that stifle the soul of man and take him further and further away from the grass that is our heritage, Wales ablaze with burning holiday cottages, the unsolved Lord Lucan mystery and continued confusion about the decimalisation system. All I can say is as one who has always sought a meaningful, rather than ceremonial role, I can guarantee your in-tray will never be short of constructive suggestions as to how best the likes of you and me can help restore Britain to the days of Eden. Not Sir Anthony Eden, I hasten to add – rather a mess, as I recall, his brief tenure – but the other sort.

> Yours, in hope and determination
> HRH The Prince of Wales

Margaret Thatcher
10 Downing Street
London
England   5 May 1979

Dear Mrs Thatcher

Well, I would be deceiving you if I said I wasn't rather taken aback by your rise to Number 10, but let no one say Charles is a 'male' chauvinist pig. Congratulations to you, Mrs Thatcher, and to your husband Denis, who I suppose will have to boil his own breakfast egg from now on.

I must say, I was impressed by your quoting from St Francis of Assisi at Downing Street – how did it go? Where there is discord let us bring . . . well, cord! I'm hoping this will be a continuing theme of your period in office after all the adversarial strife we've been suffering. Let the 1980s be all about working together: yourself, the Monarchy, in particular those of us looking for a role within it. One thing I hope we see eye to eye on is the blasted new buildings they keep erecting across London, blighting the view and adding to a sense that the national soul is settling into some sort of cement-like torpor. I trust that under Mrs Thatcher, the property developer will get short shrift!

If there is to be a keynote word to what historians will call 'The Thatcher Years', I hope and believe it will be this: compost. Do you take an interest in compost? I have yet to meet anyone, certain members of my family apart, who appears not to do so. Let us meet at the earliest possible opportunity and talk compost.

> Yours, in fellow leadership
> HRH The Prince of Wales

Margaret Thatcher
10 Downing Street
London
England   10 August 1987

Dear Mrs Thatcher   .

As you know, the problem of the inner cities continues to gnaw at the very vitals of the body politic and plays havoc with the soul of this country. Forgive me, but I must speak plainly: we must show these people that we are very, *very* concerned and will strive to be as concerned as humanly possible. I suggest we use this sentiment as a platform, an action plan to move forward and actually do something concrete, though not involving actual concrete (which is at the heart of the whole problem, if you ask me).

It occurs to me, your name is Thatcher, so thatching must be in your blood. Suppose the soul-less slate and lead of modern roofs were to be replaced with a thatched alternative? This little taste of the warp and weft of a vanished England reintroduced to the very heart of our conurbations could prove a tremendous fillip to the wretches who have to live in such ghastly places. I'm sure you could lend your generations of family expertise to such an initiative; it could be the making of your legacy. Imagine, instead of being remembered as 'Margaret Thatcher, Milk Snatcher', you'd be 'Margaret Thatcher, Thatcher'.

Yours, constructively
HRH The Prince of Wales

Margaret Thatcher
10, Downing Street
London
England   16 August 1987

Dear Mrs Thatcher

Today I received a letter from one of your fellows, which beneath the usual Civil Service oil, effectively advised me to go boil my head. His gist was that you, Mrs Thatcher, had no time available to act as 'period roofing consultant'. Can you not make time? From my end, I know I can.

Yours, etc.
HRH The Prince of Wales

John Major
10 Downing Street
London
England   29 November 1990

Dear Mr Major

Well, congratulations, of course, on reaching Number 10, but I know you'll forgive me when I say that until a few weeks ago I hadn't the faintest idea who you were. I know the last time we did meet, you had one of those identity laminates clipped to your breast pocket, which was jolly helpful. I'd advise you, for the time being at least, to hang on to that laminate, particularly when at the Palace. My grandmother is not good with new faces – catching sight of you approaching down the corridor she's likely to take you for an official from her bank and go scurrying off to her quarters to camp out until one of her gentlemen-in-waiting sounds the all-clear.

The best of luck – in your in-tray, you will find a number of initiatives and suggestions which I submitted to your predecessor, who sadly never found the time to give them her fullest attention. I trust your sense of priority is more attuned with the needs of our kingdom than hers.

> Yours, in hope and faith
> HRH The Prince of Wales

PS I did get your name right, didn't I? I'm suddenly plagued by this inkling you're called 'Geoff'. Ah, well!

John Major
10 Downing Street
London
England   12 July 1996

Dear Mr Major

I must say, I was impressed by your 'Cones hotline' initiative –
it's the sort of lead we hope our politicians will take, although
alas, all too often fail to do so. I assure you my staff are on
constant 'Cone Alert' with a large jotter in my office available
for them to write down any infractions spotted on their travels.
So far, it would seem from glancing at its pages that there is
nothing to report, which suggests the motorway people have
already taken heed of your scheme.

    I wonder if I could run by you an initiative of my own: a
five-point plan to get Britain back on its feet, which, although
'apolitical' in nature could, with your support I hope, become
official government policy, or at least form the general basis for
policy. It runs as follows:

    SOCKS: Pull them up!
    PECKER: Keep it up!
    IDEAS: Buck them up!
    CHINS: Keep them up!
    EARS: Prick them up!

    If you read down the left-hand side, it forms the mnemonic
'SPICE', which seems to be a buzzword at the moment. I'm
sure you'll agree, as a man who wants to get things done
himself, it's a catch-all corrective against pessimism, despair,
cynicism, spinal curvature of the soul, slacking and slouching.
So, once your men in suits have put some flesh on these bones,
shall we clear our respective diaries to make a joint
announcement? I'll raise another alert among my staff.

            Yours, 'on the hotline'
            HRH The Prince of Wales

John Major
10 Downing Street
London
England   14 July 1996

Dear Mr Major

Pulling back in the Bentley towards the Palace, I spotted a cone!
It was lying on the pavement, next to an abandoned shopping
trolley. Possibly the result of student 'high jinks', but thought
you should know all the same.

>   Yours, etc.
>   HRH The Prince of Wales

John Major
10 Downing Street
London
England   16 July 1996

Dear Mr Major

Has anything been done about that cone? I need something in
writing for my records.

>   Yours
>   HRH The Prince of Wales

Tony Blair
10 Downing Street
London
England   3 May 1997

Dear Mr Blair

Well, I must congratulate you, of course. Labour in power, eh? That used to mean smelly pipes, beer and sandwiches; also trade union leaders shambling in and out of Number 10, representing members whose 'jobs', sadly, mostly involved filling the atmosphere with ghastly industrial effluvium.

You, I sense at a glance, are different: you remind me of myself as a younger man. A moderniser, impatient with the old dogmas, eyes blazing with ambition, tough on things, tough on the causes of things . . . I like that. I sense we can work together. I have not always felt able to make the same sort of connection with your predecessors but with you I feel confident enough to say that when you are eventually relieved of office, you could perhaps work with me as a senior advisor on my staff. Yes, I believe that's how much we see eye to eye on things (and the causes of things).

Yours, millennially
HRH The Prince of Wales

Tony Blair
10 Downing Street
London
England   11 March 2005

Dear Mr Blair

Concerning the Eurovision Song Contest, then. As you know, this is an important gala occasion, perhaps on a par with the annual Royal Variety Show, in which the best and brightest European songwriting talent 'battle it out' under the bright lights. My staff and I tune in every year — it's their annual treat.

However, in recent years the United Kingdom has fallen behind. This does no good to our credibility as a trading partner. Hang it all, at this rate we'll get fewer and fewer foreign orders, more and more jobs will be lost and there'll be more and more 'boys in the hoods' on street corners.

I feel it's my duty to take a lead and so I've taken it upon myself to pen some 'lyrics' to which music could be set with a view to entering the Contest. I'd like your honest opinion.

Paean to This Green Jewel of Mine

Merrie, Merrie Englande
Where stout yeomen and apple-cheeked wenches caper round yon maypole
Where hope lies, like the turnip, in the soil
Where the farmhand, like the slug, is happy with his lot
Where the herbs that flourish in yon hedge cure all that ails thee

And where the church bells ring out their Song Of Pleasantness

Bing Bing-a-Bong, Bing Bing-a-Bong

Bing Bong-a-Bong, Bing Bing-a-Bong

Bing Bing-a-Bong, Bing Bing-a-Bong
Bing Bong-a-Bong, Bing Bing-a-Bong

(repeat several times)

The last bit I slipped in to 'jazz it up' a bit for the young ones. As for musical accompaniment, may I make a bold suggestion: that you yourself, as a guitarist of note, compose a melody? It would certainly be a demonstration of Government and Monarchy really working together for their subjects. Could you let me have your reply, with sheet music sample, within 48 hours?

Yours, in tune
HRH The Prince of Wales

Gordon Brown
10 Downing Street
London
England   28 June 2007

Dear Mr Brown

So, at last you have your moment in the sun. I, too, know what it is to be kept around waiting, waiting and waiting, despite one's expectations as a young man and the sense that the person incumbent was holding on for as long as they could because they suspected the fellow champing at the bit to take over was some sort of dundering incompetent.

And with those comforting words, I wish you well in what will doubtless be a long and successful tenure in office.

Yours, in fellow stewardship
HRH The Prince of Wales

Leaders of Britain (For a Short While)

David Cameron
10 Downing Street
London
England   12 May 2010

Dear Mr Cameron

So, now that you and Clegg have thrashed things out, I can
finally extend congratulations on your partial electoral success.
It's not to everyone's liking in this so-called meritocratic age
that an old Etonian has his hands on the keys to Downing
Street but between you and me, better an Eton man than a
Gordonstoun one (or certainly some of those who came to
manhood via that particular institution, in which sadism
among boys was practically part of the curriculum).

As you hover on the threshold of governmental
responsibility I see in your fresh face and rosy cheeks the
perhaps naive optimism of a young lad who fetched up for his
first term at Gordonstoun. His name too was David. I forget
his surname – I was later given to understand that he would, in
time, have been groomed to fag for me. But this was never to
be. I remember in the dining hall some of the fourth form boys
were discussing putting on some sort of Christmas cabaret
whereupon David – who had been sitting adjacent to them –
interjected, trilling about how at his prep school he had 'done
a turn', singing 'Food, Glorious Food' from the musical *Oliver!*
This, to my mounting horror, he proceeded to demonstrate in
a soprano that carried across the hall.

As a public schoolboy I need hardly remind you, Mr
Cameron, that no one likes a chatty little swine, especially a new
bug – but a singing one? Like a close escort of some hapless
victim of Stalin's purges summarily removed from the Star
Chamber, the fourth formers took him out of the hall and into
the boys lavatories where, by all accounts, they gave him such a

fearful roughing-up that he was under the care of Matron for three days before his father did what I wish mine had done — which is to say, drove up to the school in his Rolls and whisked him away for good, leaving the housemaster with a piece of his mind into the bargain.

That was the Gordonstoun way and I trust it's not the Eton way. I like what you say about compassionate Conservatism. I, too, dream of presiding over a kingdom in which one's subjects do not suffer bullying, ear-tweaking, ragging or urination in lunchboxes. At a glance, I can see that had you gone to Gordonstoun, you would have been what we called a 'roastee', not a 'roaster'.

> Yours, in sympathy
> HRH The Prince of Wales

David Cameron
10 Downing Street
London
England   12 May 2010

Dear Mr Cameron

It just came to me: Partington. That was his name, David Partington — no idea what became of him. Well, carry on, eh? Those essential public services won't cut themselves!

> Yours, etc.
> HRH The Prince of Wales

Leaders of Britain (For a Short While)

David Cameron
10 Downing Street
London
England   13 October 2010

Dear Mr Cameron

Pootling through Central London in my official car, I was
deeply conscious of how slow our progress was, which was the
dickens of an annoyance as I was late for my appointment at the
Federation For Corporate Concern's annual conference. I was
due to deliver a keynote speech entitled, 'There You Are, My
Man – The Importance of Giving a Little Back'.

   As we sat in gridlock, I did, however, spot a remarkable
sight – that of enterprising young men pulling around
tourists in brightly painted rickshaws for a token fee. I felt
like I'd been blessed with a vision of the future and I invite
you, Mr Cameron, as a man of the future, to implement it.
Suppose commuters formed a 'rickshaw pool' in which, say,
one man pulled two of his colleagues to work, only for each
of them to reciprocate over the coming days? The Cabinet
could take a lead.

   The next time I'm being driven through London it would
be tremendous to have my chauffeur wind the window down,
enabling me to see you cheerfully pulling Mr Clegg and Mr
Osborne along to Parliament, with Mr Osborne returning the
favour to you and Mr Clegg the next day, and Mr Clegg taking
his turn the day after that. You could call yourselves 'the
jambusters'! Of course Mr Eric Pickles presents a problem but
perhaps he could be declared exempt from the scheme on the
grounds of circumference.

           Practically, yours
           HRH The Prince of Wales

David Cameron
10 Downing Street
London
England   10 November 2010

Dear Mr Cameron

Time was, you know, Cameron, when a politician wasn't a
politician unless he had the sort of beard a small bird could nest
in! Sadly, those days are past. You yourself, it seems, are the 'new
model'. During our conversations at close quarters I have been
fascinated to study your face. It's as if you are made of silicone.
Have you ever shaved? Do you have some bizarre skin condition?
In which case I apologise for bringing the subject up.

　　How long do you think it would take you to grow a beard?
My wife reckons about twelve months but I'm inclined to think
anything between two and three years. This is not flippancy — I
wouldn't take up your valuable time with this issue were I not
genuinely intrigued.

　　　　　Yours, in anticipation
　　　　　HRH The Prince of Wales

Tony Blair
Houses Of Parliament
London
England   3 July 2011

Dear Mr Blair

I know you're no longer an 'MP' but I suppose they'll be glad to
forward your mail after all that you did for parliament.

　　I must say, I'm astonished to read what your sidekick

Campbell has to say in his diaries about my excessive and interfering letter writing. He wasn't confusing me with either Andrew or Edward, was he? Off the top of my head, I'm hard pressed to remember any letters I wrote to you at all. Yes, there was China, and fox hunting, oh yes, and the whole GM foods question, I grant you, and the hereditary peers business I now recall, and, ah yes, Europe, nuclear power, the role of the loom in the so-called 'service economy', the one about yoghurt, one written in error intended for the 'hoofer' Lionel Blair, one in which I sent you some cuttings of limp parsley acquired from one of our ghastly supermarket chains asking what was to be done, several demanding why your deputy, portly fellow, name escapes me, senior moment, my apologies . . . ah yes, Prescott! — why Prescott hadn't yet replied to my letters and requesting you to give him a 'nudge' and perhaps no more than a couple of hundred others. Other than that, none at all, to my knowledge.

What irks me is that you never brought it up with me yourself. In our meetings, you were rather apt to regard me in that boggle-eyed way of yours, with that rictus expression clamped to your chops as if you had smiled too much as a child and your face had set that way. I'm sorry, that isn't a facial affliction, is it? I made a similar 'gaffe' once with Gordon Brown and his eyeball.

> Wounded, yours
> HRH The Prince Of Wales

PS — I resent this insinuation of your fellow Campbell that I am somehow out of touch and elitist. I should say that I would never, never ask anyone to do anything that I, myself, would not ask my manservant to do.

The Beat Musicians: Those Who Make Us Swivel to the Rhythm

The Beatles
Parlophone Records
London
England   13 April 1963

Dear Beatles

I don't really like 'pop' music because even though it has a good rhythm, it seems a bit silly and repetitive, and just for girls who are into fashion. But The Beatles are something different. I don't know what it is about you, but I find myself humming your songs and sometimes even snapping my fingers when I hear your tunes – they're 'catchy', 'man'!

I've decided I really don't want to be a prince; I think I'd really rather be a Beatle. I wonder if any of you would care to do my job? I was thinking of you in particular, Ringo: you're only the drummer, that's the easiest instrument; I could manage that. And you get to sit down during the concert, which the others don't! You could swap places with me, Ringo – you could do my job, I'm sure of it. I'm very grown-up and serious about this, intensely serious. Not like I was with Tommy Steele, this is serious. Tomorrow, I'm going to ask my mother and father if we can swap. Will you ask your mother and father too, Ringo? You'd be king one day – King Ringo the First. I want to meet girls.

Yours
(Soon to be ex?) HRH The Prince of Wales

John Lennon and Yoko Ono
Amsterdam Hilton Hotel
Amsterdam
The Netherlands   13 April 1969

Dear Mr Lennon and Miss Ono

I hope you don't consider this correspondence an intrusion,
nor that you are required to get out of bed in order to fetch it,
thus scuppering your whole 'gimmick'. I expect you have people
to do that sort of thing for you, anyway. Being idealists, I don't
suppose you believe in Princes and suchlike, but I trust you
have nothing against Wales and so on that basis we can meet
halfway.

    This 'Go to bed rather than make war' idea of yours is jolly
fine, I think in principle, but as a young man on the point of
carrying out my family's long tradition of military service, I
don't believe I can in my heart of hearts advocate loafing to that
extent. Perhaps if you were to compromise — if you could adjust
your message so that it was something like 'Be sure to get a
good, peaceful night's sleep' then I could cheerfully give it the
Royal seal of endorsement. With the amount of rushing about
in the modern world, 'shut-eye' is on the decline, I'm sure we
might agree. Could we not work together on this?

        Your humble servant
        HRH The Prince of Wales

    PS On a lighter note, when I heard The Beatles might be
splitting up, my first reaction was 'Oh, no!' — think about it!

Johnny Rotten
Virgin Records
London
England   17 May 1977

Dear Mr Rotten

Senior palace officials advise me not to make contact with you
in this way but I have done so nonetheless and so I hope I might
appeal to what I believe to be the vestige of decency you have in
you and keep this correspondence between ourselves. I think if
the Royals are to modernise, we must not be 'aloof' but keep
'channels of communication' open between oneself and 'street-
fighting toughs' like you.

I realise you're an 'angry young man' – I get angry myself
sometimes, so I know exactly how you feel – but I understand
you plan to release your punk disc 'God Save The Queen' to
coincide with my mother's Jubilee celebrations. Regretfully, in
a democracy I cannot ask you to suppress your free speech.
Might I then suggest that instead of attacking my mother on
this, her most special occasion, that I place myself in her stead?
Write a punk song about me instead, if you really must get
things off your chest. I can take the brickbats. It might run as
follows:

> God bless the Prince
> Let's make him into mince
> He's got stupid stick-out ears
> Gets his kicks shooting deers.

If that last line doesn't work, my brother Prince Andrew,
whom I took into my confidence, suggests, 'His friends are all
queers'. I think he himself is going through a 'punk rock'
phase – that is a revolting slander and it appalls me to think this

is the sort of thing my brother obviously believes you might write and if that's what it takes to 'seal the deal', I will fall on that particular sword but how could you be thought to think such a thing?

Yours, in secret
HRH The Prince of Wales

The Three Degrees
c/o Motown Records
Los Angeles
California
United States of America   15 November 1978

A bit of 'guesswork' on my part, sending this to the Tamla Motown address. It may well not be where you make your records at all, but I'm sure Diana Ross, if she discovers this letter the way she legendarily discovered Michael Jackson, will be kind enough to pass it on.

I must admit I hesitate to put pen to paper – to sully these sheets, as it were – but following your truly extraordinary performance at my 30th birthday party, I felt I had to convey to you the depths of feeling you stirred in me. I'm not a music 'critic' so I can't put my finger on it – whether it's the fact that there are three of you ladies, the way you seem to heat up a room with your presence, or those terrific rhythms which seem to affect one somewhere below the head and above the knees, you are a credit both to your gender and to the 'soul' community in general.

I just wish there was some way we could put our heads together on one of my pet projects: what are your views on the Preservation of the Royal Yacht, the National Fruit Collection, bio-degradable Wellington boots? Perhaps you might get involved in all three between you, one Degree per project. Take your pick, ladies!

> Yours, in a sort of canine devotion
> HRH The Prince of Wales

The Village People
New York
USA   6 May 1979

You may remember that I wrote to you before following the success of your hit disc, 'YMCA'. I remember saying to you that while discotheque was, and still isn't, my sort of thing, you clearly had a knack of combining exhortation with entertainment, which almost certainly accounted for your huge success among young people. I advised you, you'll recall, to target your songwriting skills towards the Armed Services, who are always short of new recruits, and I was immensely gratified when you took up my suggestion with your 'follow-up' song, 'In The Navy', which was as much of a success as its predecessor.

I hope you don't mind my scratching my chin a bit doubtfully, but if I might venture a criticism, it is that the accompanying promotional film may have given a misapprehension of 'life at sea' for the fresh cadet. For a start when piped aboard you are not greeted by men in hard hats, police caps or Red Indian headdresses. There is no unsupervised semaphore disco dancing on deck. Rather, one must first undergo early morning drill from a gunnery instructor, acquaint oneself with the rudiments of Morse code and learn how to navigate picket boats into pontoons. None of this features in your film and it is, I regret to say, the poorer for it. An opportunity missed, but we can move forward together and learn from our mistakes.

Yours, man to man
HRH The Prince of Wales

Stevie Wonder
c/o Motown Records
Los Angeles
California   18 August 1979

Dear Mr Wonder

How does it work when you get correspondence? Do your people translate it into Braille? (I'm afraid none of my people have Braille). Or does someone read it out loud to you? This concerns me as there will be a temptation, this being a letter from me, for whoever reads it to do so in a 'Charles voice', which can end up sounding inadvertently comical.

Well, that can't be helped. I was writing to congratulate you on your latest album, *Journey Through The Secret Life Of The Plants*. A lot of the so-called, self-styled 'critics' have scratched their heads at this remarkable 'double gatefold album' and even wondered aloud if you were under the influence of certain substances when you wrote it. However, you, like me, have vision (I say, I'm awfully sorry, that didn't come out at all right but you know what I mean). I confidently predict *The Secret Life Of The Plants* will be remembered long after all your other works, such as *Songs In The Key Of Life*, have been forgotten. I thank you for this work – and, may I say, the plants thank you also.

Yours, in horticultural appreciation
HRH The Prince of Wales

Adam Ant
c/o CBS Records
London
England   17 September 1981

Dear Mr Ant

It's been hard to avoid your song, 'Prince Charming', which currently sits at Number One in the hit parade. I regret to say that whenever my brothers Edward or Andrew see me in the corridor, they strike up with a low, jeering chant of 'Prince Charlie, Prince Charlie', based on the tune to your disc — I suppose they think it's funny.

    May I correct you, however, on one specific point? In your lyrics, you say, 'Ridicule, ridicule is nothing to be scared of'. I can assure you, from my experiences at Gordonstoun, that it very much is. Any chance you could amend the offending words before next week's edition of *Top of the Pops*?

            Yours, constructively
            HRH The Prince of Wales

Phil Collins
Virgin Records UK
London
England   16 October 1981

Dear Mr Collins

I wonder if you could settle a bet between my father and me? I insist the words to your song are, 'I can feel it coming in the air tonight'. He contends the last bit goes 'Coming in the heir tonight'. Which of us is right? He is being rather 'leery' about it and it's upsetting my wife.

> Yours, urgently
> HRH The Prince of Wales

'Prince'
Paisley Park Studios
Minneapolis
United States of America   4 April 1987

Dear 'Prince'

As you are no doubt aware, 1987 marks the 35th anniversary of my mother's accession to the British throne. To mark the occasion, I struck on the idea of a pop concert to take place at Buckingham Palace – but a concert with a difference. My wheeze was to give the thing a royal 'theme', as reflected in the selection of artists.

And so, with the help of one of my staff (and no help, I should add, from my wife, who mistrusts my instincts in these matters – *I'll* show her!), I came up with a shortlist. It comprises:

> Prince (yourself)
> Princess (the singer of 'Say I'm Your Number One' by the songwriting firm of Stock Aitken Waterman)
> Queen
> King (you know their disc, 'Love And Pride', I take it?)

What I thought was that we might arrange the sequence of turns according to Royal hierarchy. However, my staff have already 'put out feelers' to Princess, whose people have expressed misgivings about her appearing bottom of the bill. Apparently, it's considered 'demeaning' in showbiz 'circles'. So, I wondered if you would open instead? My governess taught me that a little gentleman should always accede to a lady's wishes (not that I'm saying you are little).

So, what I thought is that you could kick things off with a half-hour set commencing about 8.15pm British time, followed by Princess, with Queen penultimately taking the stage and finally, and fittingly, King topping the bill. If that sounds amenable, do please have your people contact mine. No fee – all monies to The Prince's Trust – but lashings of tea and unlimited Battenberg cake.

> Yours
> HRH (The actual) Prince of Wales

Sinéad O'Connor
Chrysalis Records
London
England   12 February 1990

Dear Miss O'Connor

Before congratulating you on your latest hit single, one thing I must first establish – your hair, or rather lack of it. This is not due to some illness I have not been made aware of? I thought I'd ask straight off so as not to 'put my foot in it'.

Anyway, I must say, this song of yours, 'Nothing Compares 2 U' – I happened to catch it on the television set and was most struck by your performance to camera. You have the knack of making a fellow who had no part in whatever it was that caused

your unhappiness to nonetheless feel a bit of a 'heel'. I wanted to ask, though — are those tears real, or do you simply have the ability to 'turn on the waterworks' at will? Is that something you ladies can do? It would be most useful to know, the next time my own wife's eyes turn moist after some little contretemps so I can satisfy myself that she is in fact 'putting it on'.

Incidentally, I find myself in the curious situation of being 'in' with the group Status Quo. If you wish, I could arrange for you to support them on one of their upcoming tours — it would be great exposure for an 'up and coming' artist.

Yours, in assistance
HRH The Prince of Wales

Liam Gallagher
Oasis
Manchester
England   16 August 1996

Dear Mr Gallagher

Actually, even as I write, I'm not quite sure if you're the Gallagher brother I wish to be addressing. I would check with a member of my staff, but they're already much too hard pressed with other important work to be distracted by frivolities such as this. If you are the wrong brother, I'm sure you'll get wind during the course of this letter and be good enough to pass it on to the brother I am clearly talking to. One hesitates to talk of monkeys and organ grinders . . . Well, you know my meaning.

I'd like to extend my warmest felicitations on your fine compositions, 'Wonderwall' and the one with 'Champagne' in the title. I don't suppose you necessarily relish the Royal seal of approval (as a dedicated punk rocker, you'd probably spit in my face or something!), which is why I'm corresponding from a safe distance.

The reason I congratulate you is this. It has in the past been the complaint of many a father and, indeed, husband, on being made to sit through *Top of the Pops* that firstly, what they play isn't music, it's just noise, and secondly, that you can't tell the girls from the boys. My father, Prince Philip, made the same complaint when looking in on Anne and me watching the same programme in the 1960s and I found myself repeating the same complaint in the 1980s. However, here we are in the 1990s. I watch you and I can tell it's just good old-fashioned music, like the good old days. And I can very much tell who are the boys and who are the girls: you're all boys. This, I feel, is progress and you should be proud of yourselves. Keep it up!

Yours, pleasingly unconfused
HRH The Prince of Wales

The Spice Girls
c/o Virgin Records
London
England   3 November 1997

Dear Spice Girls

I must admit, in the heat of our encounter I was rather flustered and didn't quite catch which of you was which, though 'Ginger Spice' was unmistakable! I'm writing to commend you for really putting Britain on the map – it's a long time since Britannia was considered 'cool' and I expect I'm in some way to blame for that, though I strive daily to attain that condition of tepidity so oddly valued by today's young people. (What do you think it is about me – the kilts, the concern?)

And now, a delicate matter: amid the cameras and jostling I

was all too keenly aware of kisses being planted on my cheeks and even of my hindquarters being pinched (by Ginger and, I believe, Black Spice? I'm sorry – I'm not au fait with your 'soubriquets'). All of this was of course most improper, if somewhat flattering, and I certainly felt anything but cool in the midst of it all, particularly under the collar!

But my serious point is this: certain sweet nothings, I recall, were whispered in my ear. If they were meant in earnest, I must at once nip in the bud any cherished hopes on the part of any of you ladies, lovely as you are, of a liaison. Had I been many years younger, my late Uncle Dickie might have encouraged me to 'horse around' with the lovely likes of yourselves prior to any serious betrothal but I am an older man, with a serious role to play in the administration of our Kingdom, and cannot afford to have that undermined by an ill-judged choice of bride. Spirituality and Gravitas, not Sporty, not Baby, must be my watchwords.

> Yours respectfully, but alas, also distantly
> HRH The Prince of Wales (Now Spoken For)

Liam Gallagher
Oasis
Manchester
England   6 January 1998

Dear Mr Gallagher

You know, having caught a 'five-star' review in a magazine called *Q*, which one of my staff left lying around, I decided to give your latest long-playing disc a play. I must confess, even to my conservative ears it sounded as if you were rather 'playing it safe'.

Have you ever listened to the group Status Quo? Even

though their recordings essentially sound the same, they have a knack of making each new disc ever so slightly different from the last. Could you not, perhaps, take a leaf out of their book?

Yours, constructively
HRH The Prince of Wales

Robbie Williams
c/o EMI Records
London
England   6 January 2003

Dear Mr Williams

I'm looking to really 'pep up' my latest Prince's Trust line-up. In the past, I've had Phil Collins (who is always game and I suppose I shall keep him on), but who nowadays reminds of some faithful but elderly beater struggling to keep up, thrashing weakly through the grass long after the grouse have rocketed.

What I'm looking for is some 'fresh meat' or 'blood'. I need a younger act, who in their original use of beat rhythms and lyrics makes the young feel invigorated and refreshed, reminds us that we live in challenging, but optimistic times and that tomorrow belongs to our youth. In other words, someone who really fires us up the way The Beatles once did, once upon a time.

It's a shame there's no one around like that presently, don't you feel? But the search goes on — meanwhile, until I track down such a 'turn', I wonder if you yourself would care to be on 'stand-by'?

Yours, and so forth
HRH The Prince of Wales

The Beat Musicians

Sir Elton John
c/o Watford Football Club
London
England   12 January 2006

Dear Sir Elton

Congratulations on your betrothal or should I say 'partnership'.
I must admit, it was quite a personal shock when it came out
several years ago that you were a homosexual after songs like
'Crocodile Rock' and 'Saturday Night's Alright for Fighting' and
albums such as *Captain Fantastic And The Brown Dirt Cowboy*, but I am
quite accepting of it all now. Of course, I have nothing within
reason against homosexuals. Many of my grandmother's staff,
although not similarly persuaded did know, or know of, many
men who were. I know your people have been through very
difficult times in recent years despite the remarkable, almost
excessive cheerfulness you collectively maintain.

　Just a matter of protocol: this upcoming event at Highgrove
to which you and your 'plus one' are cordially invited, how
should you be announced? I was thinking, 'Your Royal
Highness, Lords, Ladies and Gentlemen, Mr and Mr Elton
John'. Is that right? It is important to get these things correct,
I feel.

　　　Yours, in acceptance
　　　HRH The Prince of Wales

Madonna/Celine Dion
c/o MTV
Los Angeles
California
United States of America   20 April 2008

Dear Misses Madonna/Dion

I trust you don't mind my addressing you jointly: it seemed
more practical and would convey that I am speaking to the both
of you with one voice, not addressing either of you as I wouldn't
the other. This concerns a recent report by an ancestry 'website'
that both you, Ms Ciccone and you, Ms Dion, may well be
related to me via my wife, the Duchess of Cornwall. It seems
there is a common, though distant lineage dating back to one
Zacharie Cloutier, a French carpenter who settled in Canada in
the seventeenth century.

Now, as you read the article through, it's clear the ancestral
connection is so bally tenuous as to be barely worth
mentioning. Obviously the authors are bent on 'mischief-
making' against the Royal Family. Some might say I should
simply ignore this sort of thing but I'm convinced it's all part of
a 'drip, drip, drip' process that threatens to erode the
Monarchy and really must be nipped in the bud, if our
institutions are to be preserved.

To this end, I've drafted an open letter to the media, to
which I hope you will both attach your names at the bottom so
that we can once and for all scotch this nonsense:

> We, the undersigned, wish to make clear any link between
> ourselves and the Royal Family is both spurious and tenuous.
> Headlines in which our names are bracketed with that of His
> Royal Highness The Prince Charles, whose tenacity and
> vision for Britain we both greatly admire, are thoroughly

frivolous and threaten to undermine the good work he does for his many good causes, such as Young British Enterprise and freer access to holistic medical treatment.

We are pop stars (and perfectly alright if you like that sort of thing) but hang it all, we're not Royalty and we never will be.

If you wish to make minor alterations, by all means run them by my staff but if I hear nothing from you in the next twenty-four hours, I'll give it the 'go-ahead' as written. *Qui tacet consentire*, as my Latin master used to say.

> Yours, expectantly
> HRH The Prince of Wales

Dave Lee Travis
c/o Radio 1
The British Broadcasting Corporation
London
England   1 June 2008

Dear Mr Travis

I write to you because I need advice from a younger disc jockey and your name sprang to mind.

I was looking to book Britney Houston for one of my Prince's Trust concerts. However, when I raised this with my sons, both of them shook their heads and left the room. Is she no longer 'in'? I thought she was quite popular.

> Yours, in puzzlement
> HRH The Prince of Wales

'Bono'
c/o U2 HQ
Amsterdam
Holland   16 July 2008

Dear 'Bono'

I'm sending this to Holland – I understand that is where you have relocated for business purposes. I've had a flash of inspiration and thought I would dash it off on paper before some high-handed Palace official talks me out of it.

I admire the bluntness of your colleague Mr Bob Geldof, who, like you, wishes to 'Make Poverty History'. The message to the 'masses' is a plain and simple one: Give us your money. Words are not enough – action is needed and that is the action required.

Here's what I envisage – a philanthropic gathering of myself (Prince Charles), yourself (Bono), Richard Branson and Bill Gates. We pose for a photo, to be published in the form of a poster to be stuck up all over Britain and beyond. It shows us standing shoulder to shoulder, staring the onlooker squarely in the eye, with our hands outstretched and imploring. And above us, in bold typeface, the words, 'GIVE US YOUR MONEY'. And beneath us, the words, 'WE NEED IT NOW!'.

It's that simple. No waffle, and no reams of gobble-de-gook about Third World this and that, just the basic message in a nutshell. I'll have my people compare diaries with yours first thing in the morning.

Yours
'Charlo' (I'm joking, of course) HRH The Prince of Wales

The Beat Musicians

Lady Gaga
c/o Universal Music
Los Angeles
California
United States of America   11 November 2009

Dear Lady Gaga

First off, one thing I must ascertain at once – you are indeed a
lady, aren't you? I don't mean of noble breeding, I'm with-it
enough to understand that in your case the 'Lady' thing is a
conceit and that you're not truly laying claim to being one of
the Hampshire Gagas – I mean an actual, physical lady. One
cannot be too careful, I find, in this day and age, and feel it's
best to make discreet preliminary enquiries.

If you are not a lady, then I trust that, as a gentleman, you
will not reveal this correspondence ever took place. However,
if you happen to be one, then do write back as I have a
proposition to put to you concerning one of our 'Outward
Bound' events. You'll agree that all of us, whether lady or
gentleman, could do with more fresh air in our lungs.

  Yours faithfully
  HRH The Prince of Wales

Lady Gaga
c/o Universal Music
Los Angeles
California
United States of America   1 December 2009

Dear Lady Gaga

I received a return of correspondence from one of your people,
which in its tone was implicitly sceptical about my bona fides.
In view of this, I must declare all future correspondence
between us to be closed. I am not accustomed to accusations
of being a 'hoaxer'.

You see, unlike yourself, I am what I purport to be: I am a
prince. And I see what you are doing by calling yourself 'Lady'
but you forget that some of us have long memories. We
remember, for example, Ray Alan and Lord Charles, the
ventriloquist double-act. So you see, you may think you are
doing something 'shocking' and 'original' by subversively
affecting to be a member of the nobility for entertainment
purposes but it is nothing new. The aristocracy may be in
decline, but it survived Lord Charles and it will survive your
onslaught also.

Yours
His Royal Highness The Prince Charles Philip Arthur
George, Prince of Wales, KG, KT, GCB, OM, AK,
QSO, PC, ADC, Earl of Chester, Duke of Cornwall,
Duke of Rothesay, Earl of Carrick, Baron of Renfrew,
Lord of the Isles and Prince and Great Steward of
Scotland

The Beat Musicians

Bob Geldof
35–38 Portman Square
London
England   30 June 2010

Dear Mr Geldof

I'm not writing to you in your capacity as a 'pop star' but then, I
suppose, few if any do nowadays. Rather, I was thinking, with it
being the 25th anniversary of Live Aid, I watched once more
the Wembley Stadium extravaganza you and your friends put
on. I must say, it was dashed embarrassing – was that really my
haircut back then? – but my heart went out once more to those
poor Ethiopians and it pains me that despite your efforts, there
are still food shortages in the Third World.

I've spoken to you before about the vital role allotments
could play in Africa – to each family, a strip of land on which
they could grow marrows, runner beans or local produce.
However, the drawback is clear: a lack of watering cans. Well
hang it all, we'll let them know it's 'Christmas Time' again and
do something about it! Let's have a national campaign to donate
unwanted watering cans to Africa. I'll set the thing in train –
I've a can that's seen better days. Bit rusty and leaky, but usable.
I'm prepared to donate it to the fighting fund. I enclose said
can – if you could pass it to the relevant African agency and get
the publicity going for more of the same, I'd be most grateful.
Doing me a favour, really, it's cluttering up my shed.

Yours, because people are dying
HRH The Prince of Wales

PS I see your middle name is Zenon. You kept that quiet
from your 'punk rocker' friends, didn't you?

Rick Parfitt
Status Quo
London
England   6 August 2010

Dear Mr Parfitt

It's funny, I must have seen you fellows play about a dozen times
during the course of my life, at various variety shows and what
have you. Wherever I go, you always seem to be booked. I'm
really not sure why, it's certainly not at my request, but there it
is – I've become strangely familiar with your oeuvre, so much so
as even the most ardent 'Quo-maniac'. Indeed, in a strange
kind of way, you've rather got under my skin.

It's clear that, like many of us now, you are in the autumn of
your years. And yet, in the moments between the slumber that
is the prerogative of us senior fellows (that, and frequent night
trips to the bathroom), I was quite taken by your onstage
gyrations. There is a sort of Shamanic quality about the
repetitive rhythms and motions of rock music, which you and
your partner, Francis Rossi, embody to the full. It's as if you're
in some sort of physical, yet spiritual communion with the
pulses of nature itself, something lost to the rest of us.

Seeing you onstage makes me realise that it's not too late for
me to learn of these pulses. By Royal Command, I therefore
summon the both of you to Highgrove, where you will teach me
the possibly ancient and healing wisdom of 'rocking'. Not all
over the world, maybe, but all over the ballroom for a start.

Yours, raring to go
HRH The Prince of Wales

The Beat Musicians

Justin Bieber
c/o MTV
Los Angeles
California
United States of America   12 November 2010

Dear Mr Bieber

As someone who takes an interest in the doings of former
members of the Commonwealth like Canada (you're always
welcome back – just ribbing!), I thought it my Sovereign duty
to congratulate you on being the most-googled person in the
world. It seems you are quite the up-and-coming young
crooner. I also read, however, rather snide remarks alleging
that in a recent interview, when asked about the 'Germans', you
professed ignorance as to who, or what, the 'Germans' were.

  Do not be upset by this – it's not such a bad thing as one
might think. A little knowledge can be a dangerous thing for a
young man. Take my son Harry. He found out at an early age
who the Germans were and without going into the sordid
detail, got himself in hot water as a result.

  And so, my advice to you is this: get on with your career,
remember to get lots of fresh air and exercise. No need to
worry your young head at this stage about the Germans,
save that knowledge for later life. It's rather complicated
and grim.

          Yours, advisedly
          HRH The Prince of Wales

Keith Richards
c/o Rolling Stones Records
London
England   28 December 2010

Dear Mr Richards

I have greatly enjoyed reading your autobiography, which my
brother Andrew bought me as a Christmas gift. He has a funny
turn of mind – he's often given to presenting me with seasonal
gifts, which he thinks I will find entirely unsuitable (last year it
was a pair of 'Speedos'. He was wrong then, and he is wrong
again this year, so once again the last laugh is on me!).

I enjoyed your account of life with the Rolling Stones,
finding it 'rich' and anecdotal. However, I was uncomfortable
with one passage in which you talked about writing to Tony
Blair and encouraging him to 'stick to his guns' over the Iraq
war. On the rights and wrongs of that conflict I make no
comment, but I would ask you: do you think it wise, as a man in
your position, to pester members of government with letters
telling them what they should or shouldn't do? They are busy
people and you, in turn, might be best advised to stick to your
own business, which is 'rocking' and 'rolling'.

Yours, constructively
HRH The Prince of Wales

The Beat Musicians

The Brothers Gibb
c/o The Bee Gees
Warner Music Group
Los Angeles
United States of America   8 January 2011

Dear Brothers Gibb

First off the bat, let me congratulate you on your continued
success in the field of discotheque, where I understand you
continue to flourish in what many consider a 'here today,
gone tomorrow' brand of popular music. And now to brass
tacks: as you must be aware, I've just published a book called
Harmony. I shan't give the plot away but essentially it's to do
with getting back to nature's own geometry, an ancient wisdom
we've lost sight of amid the smoke and soot of the industrial
age – equilateral triangles, vesicas, the golden section, you
know the sort of thing. My co-writers explain it so much
better than I do.

Anyway, I read in a periodical lying around that all the
rage these days are so-called Talking Books, or 'Audio CDs'
and what I was wondering was, it might attract readers from
the younger generation if you were to enter a recording
studio and sing certain key passages from the book in
harmony, which I understand is your forte. One Bee Gee
providing the falsetto, another the – well, you know
your business.

For your troubles, I could promise you a small
percentage of the royalties. I understand one of your
biggest hits is called 'Stayin' Alive' and hang it all, what
with the global warming and losing sight of the triangles,
'Stayin' Alive' is more important than ever for all of us on
Planet Earth, don't you feel? Speaking of which, I also
understand we are down to the last two Bee Gees so you'll

appreciate we're in a race against time to get this done while you're still with us.

> Yours, in close harmony
> HRH The Prince of Wales

Mick Jagger
c/o Rolling Stones Records
London
England   6 February 2011

Dear Mr Jagger

Aged seventeen, and in my sixth form, I was voted by unanimous ballot by my peers 'The Boy Least Likely To Turn Out Like Mick Jagger'. As 'punishment' for this supposed inadequacy, I was made to stand on my desk and perform your hit disc, 'I Can't Get No Satisfaction' – jelly legs and everything.

I have not turned out like Mick Jagger, but have *you* turned out like me? Perhaps a little, as you advance with age: you are no longer quite so wild and crazy, and a little less rubber-lipped. And, I understand you live the strenuous life with plenty of exercise. In fact, I was writing to tell you that you were the subject of an 'off-the-cuff' quip of mine: Learning of your health 'kick', I remarked that nowadays, instead of calling you Mick Jagger, they should call you 'Mick Jogger'. My staff roared – which was gratifying as they are currently under instructions not to laugh at my jokes unless they find them genuinely amusing.

> Jovially, yours
> HRH The Prince of Wales

The Royal
Household

Mummy and Daddy
Buckingham Palace
London
England   18 September 1959

Dear Mummy and Daddy

I hope you are both well. How is Anne and baby brother
Andrew? I hope they are fine. I am fine. Are the staff fine?
I hope they are fine, too.

I say, we were studying art and I read in a book about a
Frenchman who said that everyone should live in completely
glass houses – you know, like greenhouses or something. That
way, everyone could see what everyone else was doing and it
would help bring people together because they could see one
another. Don't you think it would be great if we could do that
to Buckingham Palace? I mean, instead of walls, which keep us
invisible from the people we rule over, if we could just have lots
and lots of panes of glass. That way, they could see right
through with binoculars, see what we get up to and realise we're
ordinary, down-to-earth people who care about things the same
as them and they'd be happier.

Of course, we'd keep the railings to keep toughs and rogues
from getting in and we'd keep the guards, too. But I think it's a
topping idea. Please may we do it?

> Lots of love and handshakes
> Charles

The Royal Household

HM The Queen and HRH The Prince Philip
Buckingham Palace
London
England   30 April 1962

Dear Mother and Father

By now you must be wondering how I am getting on at Gordonstoun, my new school.

Really, it is quite nice. Different from Cheam, but it seems like a good school as schools go.

I have been made welcome by the staff and am sure I will soon make friends with the other boys.

Needless to say, I am looking forward to the various activities the school has to offer.

Good food, as well — the porridge tasted quite well prepared and the tea was reasonably warm.

Masters seem quite decent sorts. Not too 'stern' or 'severe', quite strict — but that is a good thing.

Excellent desks, too: yes, as desks go, you couldn't ask for better desks. Solid, and wooden.

Have I mentioned the sports grounds? They're really quite topping. Looking forward to rugger!

Oh, and I shouldn't forget to mention the science lab, which seems very well equipped.

Masters read our letters before we send them home to check for any misspellings.

Even so, I hope you get the message about what I think of Gordonstoun!

> Please, for dear love
> Charles

Captain Mark Phillips
c/o Buckingham Palace
London
England   18 February 1973

Well, Mark

Warmest congratulations on your impending nuptials to my
sister Anne. I apologise again for declining your kind invitation
to attend the 'stag' night, but I fear I am really not much of a
'stag' person. These events seem to bring out the most feral and
atavistic tendencies in even the most civilised of men and on
such occasions I'm inclined to retreat into my shell, find a
quiet corner and reach for the Laurens van der Post volume I
always carry in my inside pocket.

　　I trust yours will be a long and happy marriage. As for
Anne, well . . . are you, Mark, familiar with the works of P.G.
Wodehouse? There's a certain sort of female he is fond of
describing in his novels: strong-willed and no-nonsense, the
sort that made Bertie Wooster quake with terror. I shan't
elaborate further except to say that I hope you, Mark, are no
Bertie Wooster.

　　Also, I note your background is equestrian. Strangely, I had
a dream last night in which you were a horse and Anne was
riding you around Hickstead – quite successfully, no faults,
until you came a cropper at the muddy brook and Anne was
plunged into murky waters. At that point I woke up, possibly in
terror. I have no idea what it all means, do you?

　　　　Yours, in impending brotherhood
　　　　Charles

The Royal Household

Diana, Princess of Wales
c/o Buckingham Palace
London
England   6 February 1982

Dear Diana

Knowing you as I do a bit, I'm sure you're going to think it's a
bit formal, my writing to you like this – especially when you're
sitting in the next room, doing whatever you're doing in there,
but sometimes I find this to be the best way of unleashing what
you might call the maelstrom of my emotions, beneath what is,
I daresay by 'Duran Duran' standards, a fuddy-duddy exterior.
To really talk about what I'm feeling, and hang all protocol and
tongue-tied small talk.

So, how are you? I'm all right. I just spoke to Anne on the
phone. She's all right. Grandmamma continues all right,
though I don't think she likes Mr Scargill. I'm all right, as I
mentioned. Are you all right? Well, all right. I hear music
coming through the walls, so I suppose you must be all
right – if anyone knows what 'all right' is.

Gosh, somehow it feels good to have got all that off my
chest.

        Your Prince
        Charles

The Prince Charles Letters

HRH The Prince Philip
Buckingham Palace
London
England   1 March 1990

I've jolly well had it, Father! I've had it up to here . . . I'm
fed up with being habitually addressed as 'boy', even though
I'm almost 42 years old, and addressed with the habitual
brusqueness even a char-wallah might bristle at. I'm fed up
with you sauntering into my quarters without knocking and
striking up conversations with my potted plants, which are
sarcastic in the extreme and in no way designed to nourish their
growth, merely for you to have a hearty laugh at my expense.

I'm fed up with your summary family meetings, which I
notice I am often the only one to come running to attend, in
which you dress me down about some supposed infraction or
other in front of the footmen. If I want to slouch at the dining
table, I'll slouch – and hang the consequences to my posture!

Most of all, I'm fed up with you regaling your old Navy
chums over brandy and cigars with tales of the privations I
suffered at Gordonstoun at the hands of bullies like Roger
Braithwaite, Tuppy Fitzroy and the Armitage brothers (G) and
(S). I deplore your bringing up the yoghurt episode, which was
one of the most traumatic and humiliating of my young life
and from which I feel, in a very real and keen sense, I have
never recovered. It appalls me to suspect your sole, beastly
motive for delivering me into the most miserable years of my
existence was so as to build for yourself a fund of amusing,
after-dinner anecdotes.

Well, now that's that out in the open, I don't suppose I'll
send this but the sentiments are deeply felt, mark my words.

Charles

The Royal Household

HRH The Prince Edward
Buckingham Palace
London
England   6 April 1991

I thought I'd entrust delivery of this letter to a footman rather than the Royal Mail, which is not always reliable, if the number of replies I expect to receive to my own correspondence that go missing is any guide.

Well, hello, Eddie! We were born rather far apart, you and me. Creates a distance, really; makes it hard to know a fellow. From that distance, however, I have wondered what it must be like to be HRH The Prince Edward: last, if by no means least of the litter, but inevitably the overlooked one. Is it like being the fourth man on the moon, the one no one's ever heard of; or that fellow Ridgeley, who used to sing alongside George Michael? In some ways I envy you, really – in terms of discharging your duties to the nation. With me, it's a constant grind of appointments, correspondence, committees, campaigns, a tremendous responsibility . . . With you, it was *It's A Knockout*. I sometimes think, suppose we could swap places? But then I think, perhaps best not. Even *It's A Knockout* proved a bit of a stretch, if I recall.

Perhaps by correspondence like this, we can draw closer.

Yours, in hope
Charles

The Prince Charles Letters

HRH Princess Margaret of York
Buckingham Palace
London
England   17 March 1993

Dear Margaret

I know we don't correspond often – I suppose we really don't
have an awful lot in common, you and me. As I was growing up,
you seemed a somewhat remote, glamorous figure, wreathed in
mystery and smoke. Whenever I get a whiff of tobacco I must
confess I always think of you, and vice-versa.

You will see that I sent you a copy of a letter dated 16
November 1992, sent to Malcolm Rifkind and circulated
among members of my family. It concerned plans to reduce the
number of regimental bands – a decision I deplore because this
would irrevocably alter the whole framework and fabric of the
British Army.

Somehow I imagine you sitting there reading that letter,
draped on a chaise longue, cigarette and gin in one hand,
exclaiming to yourself, 'Do you think I'd give two figs if I never
had to hear another bloody note by the Coldstream Guards
again? If it were up to me, I wouldn't just decommission them,
I'd have them all shot for crimes against light classical music
and personally jump up and down on their bugles! Many a
garden party they've ruined with their abysmal medleys of James
Bond theme tunes parping away in the background! I've said it
before, I'll say it again: what that boy Charles needs is some sex.
Sex, sex and oodles of it, and we'd be hearing a lot less from
him about the framework of the British Army. Sex! And he's
not getting it from that girl, that's for sure.'

I suppose I simply wanted to confirm my fears are
unfounded and you're behind me four square on this one.

> Your admiring nephew
> Charles

The Royal Household

HM The Queen
Buckingham Palace
London
England   16 October 1995

Dear Mummy

I'm writing to you for no reason in particular, but what with
it being a pleasant autumn day – 'season of mists and mellow
fruitfulness' and so on – I thought it would be nice to
correspond just for correspondence's sake.

Do you ever look at Grandmamma and wonder? She has
life pretty good, really – doesn't she? Gin, Ascot, more gin,
fine food, fine living quarters to rattle around in; able to speak
her mind about whatever she wishes with only family and a
discreet staff within 'earshot' and she can spend time with the
dogs, put her feet up, peruse the *Racing Post* . . . Makes one a
little jealous, doesn't it? Well, I suppose being retired, having
so few public duties, these are the perks. After all, at her age
she ought to be taking it easy – let the younger generation take
the reins and the responsibilities, and all that.

I understand you're to visit Barrow-in-Furness next month
to have a look around the new extension to their submarine-
building facilities. Barrow-in-Furness is so nice in November,
I imagine. Such are a monarch's duties. I wonder what
Grandmamma will be doing that afternoon? Watching the
races, I expect.

Just random thoughts, you know, on an autumn day. The
days are getting shorter, aren't they?

        Your dear eldest son
        Charles

The Prince Charles Letters

HM Queen Elizabeth The Queen Mother
Buckingham Palace
London
England   6 April 1998

'What ho, Grandmamma!' as that Bertie Wooster from those
paperbacks you like might say. I hope that strikes the right note
because the matter I'm writing to you about is one of some
delicacy.

You see, I was rattling around the Palace the other day,
kicking one's heels and chafing as one does about not having a
role, some important task in modern life. Then Father piped
up, gruffly: 'If you want something to do, how about getting
your grandmother to do something about her bloody
overdraft?' So there it is.

As you know, Grandmamma, I have always held you in the
greatest esteem. I treasure your wartime stories about dear old
Lord Halifax, champagne by candlelight in the East Wing and
poring over maps of Canada. I fondly recall your impassioned
remarks about 'that repulsive little man, bent on war and on the
ruin of all we hold dear' – though with hindsight, was that
perhaps a little unkind to Churchill?

Yours was truly the best of generations. And so I'm
appealing to the better side of your nature: if you could see
your way to reining in spending on the 'gee-gees', the gin and
the staff, and the gin and so forth, I think you'd find the people
of Britain would be inspired by your noble sacrifice as you
looked them in the face. Recently, I forewent having a
replacement toilet seat flown out by private plane to me at
Klosters and I like to think both the people and Mother Earth
thought well of me for this.

Anyway something to think about, to my mind: I'm just the
messenger, by the way. I understand you threw a shoe at the last
person who mentioned all this. Please, Grandmamma, don't

throw a shoe at me! They threw shoes at me at Gordonstoun. Rather a lot . . . The memory of those days would hurt a good deal more than the sharp end of the heel.

> Your devoted grandchild
> 'Little Big Ears' Charlie

HRH The Princess Anne
c/o Buckingham Palace
London
England   1 August 2002

Dear Anne

I suspect on receiving this, you'll stare away in that rather deadpan, mysterious way, full of distant hauteur and what have you, but I simply felt I had to open up a line of communication with you far from the stuffiness and the stiff upper lip of the family fireplace. What I wanted to say is this: invariably, when we do clink sherry glasses together, I find that I can think of little to talk to you about but horses. It may be my misapprehension, but they seem to be your sole topic of conversation – or so I assume.

I know you mock me for not knowing the difference between a fetlock and a martingale, but this seems unfair as I have a broad portfolio of interests. Can I suggest therefore that we have a sort of agreed-upon rota for subject matter when we meet, so that I get to talk about the things I'm interested in one time, then you have your turn the next. So, the rota might go like this:

> ME: Breaking out of the concrete straitjacket: moves towards the greener pastures of a British New Age . . .
> YOU: Horses.

ME: The wisdom of Sir Laurens van der Post, seer, Shaman,
   prophet, oracle in human shape . . .
YOU: Horses.
ME: Retuning the Pianoforte of the English Soul: Getting
   back to a pre-industrial harmony with Mother Nature, or
   Gaia . . .
YOU: Horses.

Of course it doesn't have to be horses — it can be whatever
you want. I put 'horses' because with you, it's all I can think of.
We could send and receive messages via some go-between — one
of my staff, or perhaps your husband.

> Yours, in great fondness
> Charles

HRH Princess Michael of Kent
Kensington Palace
London
England   4 October 2003

I trust you are well. I am essentially in good health, but a little
troubled by the most bizarre dream I had last night.

In it, I was transported back to my childhood days: we were
in the nursery. You were our strict governess — in fact, strict to
the point of being downright psychopathic. What's more, you
insisted on calling my sister Anne 'Prince Anne' and myself
'Princess Charles'. Anne seemed to rather enjoy the whole
thing, I did not.

Have you any idea what on earth all this could possibly
mean, Michael?

> Yours, in concern
> Charles

The Royal Household

HRH The Prince Harry
c/o Highgrove
Tetbury
Gloucestershire
England

13 January 2005

Well now, Windsor Minor

It would appear from a glance at the 'yellow press' Father and Son need to have something of a talk. Don't worry, it won't be like my Father-Son talks — there'll be no tweaking of short hairs or barking short sentences in which the word 'DISAPPOINTMENT!' features strongly, an inch from your face. In fact, I thought I'd best do this by correspondence.

It seems you thought it a bit of a rag to dress up as a National Socialist. You must understand the Nazis were beastly people: they bombed the East Wing, you know. It's the only reason your great grandmother could look the East End in the face — had a great effect on her. Even towards the end of her life, she watched _EastEnders_ and always looked the characters in the face; a remarkable woman, your great grandmother — a testimony to the wartime spirit. And may I say in tribute to her that neither she nor your late, great grandfather King George ever gave in to the temptation to dress up as Nazis, certainly not where cameras might be lurking. For that, we owe them so much.

In short, if you must dress up as a German, be a post-war German like Mr Helmut Kohl. I know it's not quite the same, but needs must.

Yours in kindly reproach
'Dad'

Camilla Parker Bowles
c/o Highgrove
Tetbury
Gloucestershire
England   9 April 2005

Well, my dear

You know what I'd really like to say to you, but given our
exchanges have in the past fallen into the wrong hands with
decidedly embarrassing consequences, I'll keep this note on a
friendly, but formal footing if it's all the same to you, dear
sugar lump.

Today, as you know, is the day of our Civil Wedding. Who'd
have thought it, eh, thirty years ago? And now you're Duchess
of Cornwall. I hope you don't mind – the leg end of Britain, I
know, and I can think of certain ex-wives of mine who shall be
nameless, who probably couldn't have stuck its rugged scenery
and bracing remoteness for more than a half-hour without the
need to go sit in the back of the Range Rover and listen to bally
Phil Collins on the Sony Walkman set.

But you, my dear: you are different. Hang it all, raisins
to my nuts, with you I feel I can talk about biodegradable
Wellingtons for hours without the other party rolling their
eyes as if in the presence of some dreary old prater. Not you,
dearest – we shall have many such conversations. I envisage the
remainder of our lives like some long, everlasting Sunday in
Cornwall.

Your tin whistle, 'pon which a merry tune of love you play

Charles

The Royal Household

HM The Queen
Buckingham Palace
London
England   6 January 2007

Dear Mummy

I know in the past you've said to me, 'Stop with all these letters!
If you've something to say to me, knock on my door and just say
it,' but hang it all, Mother, what with opening a swimming bath
here and receiving some foreign dignitary there, you're never
around and we never seem to get the two or three clear hours
I'd need to expand on my ideas in full.

Before you read on, yes, I'm going to talk about what I know
you think you know I'm going to talk about and well, yes, I am,
but please don't stop reading here. We've simply got to
MODERNISE. I know it's a dirty word to you, like 'knickers' or
something, but I've put it in bullet points so as to make my
points quickly and concisely:

- For a start I'm not talking about the guards replacing their
  bearskin hats with baseball hats worn backwards. Let's get
  that clear.
- Perhaps we should 'blog'. It's all the rage. I know neither you
  nor Father are keen and nor, I suppose, are the rest of the
  family but I'd be happy to take on that one. I could be the
  family representative. Maybe Edward could 'tweet'? 140
  characters would probably be about his limit.
- Would you at least consider the idea of travelling to the
  Opening of Parliament by bicycle — it would send out such
  a tremendous message. I know it's something you're
  uncomfortable with, but I'd urge you to give it a try. Perhaps
  have a 'practice run' on a bike once or twice around the
  courtyard, early in the morning when there are relatively few
  tourists around?

- Recycling bins, prominently displayed outside the railings of the Palace: one for food waste, one for glass, one for paper and so forth. We do need to be taking a lead on this one. Of course, the press would have to be 'on their honour' not to go rummaging through in the hope of unearthing something the 'red tops' would find amusing or salacious. Surely the issue here is one of trust?
- Back to that baseball hats thing, for the guards. Maybe there is some merit in it. Not worn backwards, that would just be silly – but frontways? We mustn't be seen to be 'out of touch'.

I'd simply ask you to give these ideas the time and consideration they merit – they're just a few, I have lots more. We have to think outside of the Royal box! (That is a joke, btw, which may not amuse you but certainly amuses my staff whenever they hear it.)

> Yours, moving forward
> Charles

HRH The Prince Andrew
c/o Buckingham Palace
London
England   6 August 2008

Dear Andrew

I trust you don't mind my writing to you like this for although the hour is late, the inkwell is not yet dry and I thought – well, brother to brother – we might engage in the sort of one-to-one honest exchange that is so difficult around the Palace or at functions when Mother (and particularly, Father) are around.

I've often wondered how do you feel I 'cut it' as an older

brother? Call me paranoid, but I imagine you getting off rather boisterous remarks at my expense when you're in company with your old flying chums or the fellows down at International Trade & Investment, or the Worshipful Company of Shipwrights – sly, mocking quips involving plants and ears.

Is this so, or do you harbour a grudging respect for your 'older bro', perhaps even tinged with envy? Could all this swearing and fighter pilot stuff be evidence of some inferiority complex, do you feel? If so, this is an opportunity to spill it out, confidentially. Think of me as a sort of teddy bear, yourself as the very small boy I remember you all too well as.

Yours, fraternally
Charles

HRH The Prince Andrew
c/o Buckingham Palace
London
England   8 August 2008

Dear Andrew

This is a short letter to inform you that I decided not to send you the original letter I proposed to send you, which is why you have not received it. Instead, you are receiving this one.

I hope this letter finds you well and clarifies the situation.

Yours, etc.
Charles

HM The Queen
Buckingham Palace
London
England   13 June 2010

Dear Mummy

I tried to get through to you by phone but I dropped the thing.
It sort of lay there and made a strange buzzing noise – you don't
have a bee loose at the Palace, do you? So, I thought, 'Well,
send for the inkpot instead!' I didn't just think it I said it, and
someone did.

It's – ooh, what time is it? It's about three in the afternoon,
I should think. Diary's been empty the last couple of days, so
we've rather been taking it easy down at Highgrove, kicking our
heels with a few family and friends. We were twiddling our
thumbs this morning, the old carriage clock ticking away, and
as it struck eleven, we thought, 'Hang it all! The sun's taking its
time clambering over the bally yard arm, let's break open a
bottle and really take advantage of the day!'

And so we did – we jolly well have, I mean to say. It's a
beautiful day. Is it a beautiful day in London? It's a beautiful
day here. Did I ask if it was a beautiful day in London? Oh yes,
I believe I just did. Camilla is lying on the floor giggling at
something she's seen on the ceiling. She says, 'Hullo, Your
Majesty!', by the way. That's rather friendly of her, isn't it?
She's ever such a friendly duchess. Oh dear, she's staggering to
her feet and attempting a curtsey. I think as you were, Camilla
dearest. Yes, it's a beautiful day. Is it a beautiful day in
London?

I wanted to say something to you – ah, yes, it was this. Being
in the Royal Family. Sometimes I know it can be the most
frightful bind but all in all, you know, taken in the round,

killing two birds with one stone and what have you, it's pretty
terrific really, isn't it? I mean, it could be a lot worse. A lot, lot,
lot, lot worse. I say, that's a lot of 'lots', isn't it? They look
rather funny on the page, all in a row like that, like – like little
soldiers.

And you know, Mummy, I want to thank you, thank you
personally, thank you *very* much for – well, bringing me into
this world, and not just into this world but into this lovely, *lovely*
Royal Family. It's ruddy great! Just think, there I was up in the
spirit world when you and Father happened to – well, you know,
you chose that moment to lie back and – I just happened to be
next in the queue up there. Five minutes later, just five minutes
later and I'd have been born into some other place. Or five
minutes earlier, for that matter. Just think, I could be some
Bedouin elder roasting camel dung, or some old fellow sitting
on a rusty chair in a square in Algiers, in his only pair of
trousers watching the world go by and wondering to himself,
'What the devil is THIS all about?'.

But no, you were bang on time. It was your duty, of
course. You always did your duty to your county. County? I
meant country, always country first. I admire you for
that – even when it took you off to Kenya and I had to stay
home with my toys. Country first. And now I'm a little
melancholy . . . because they don't understand us, do they?
Our enemies, I mean. The people who would have us toppled,
even after all we've done. They know who they are. Oh, they
know who they are! I wish I knew who they were, but there you
go. They're bastards, Mummy. Bastards! There, I said it.
Bastards. Our backs are against the wall and they're out to
destroy us, but we won't let them destroy us, will we, Mummy?
Not even if the rest of them have all run over to the other side
and we're the last two standing. We won't let them, won't let
them. Won't. Let. Them.

And now, I feel rather sleepy. I think I may take a little doze out on the lawn. It's a beautiful day down here. Is it a beautiful day in London?

> Yours, on a beautiful day
> 'Charlie'

PS: Who do you think would win in a fight between Andrew and me? You must have wondered – I know I have!

The British Homeopathic Association
(by email)   14 June 2010

Good morning

I find myself suffering something of a 'headache'. I was wondering, I know homeopathic remedies work on the principle of dilution but is there something you could have your lab people work up that's more in the nature of 'super-strength', just this once? Because I think that's what I need.

> Urgently, yours
> HRH The Prince of Wales

HM The Queen
(via email)   14 June 2010
Hello Mummy

As this is a matter of urgency, I am using the emergency channel of 'email'. A letter may have arrived for you this

morning in a large envelope with the misspelled word
'Buckingham' crossed out several times and a Gloucestershire
postmark. I have certain information on this from sources. I'd
urge you not to open it as it may be a letter bomb, or some
such. Simply have one of the footmen dispose of it.

> Yours sincerely
> Charles

HM The Queen
Buckingham Palace
London
England   8 November 2010

Dear Mummy

I see you have joined the twenty-first century and signed up to
Facebook! Charles 'likes' this! I rushed to my laptop and looked
on your page with great interest. However, I noted you have
barred the 'friends' facility.

I can certainly understand this, as well as your desire not to
be 'poked' – which would be a green light for all manner of
ribaldry from the Footlights brigade. I was wondering, though:
in the case of those nearest and dearest to you, could you
possibly make exceptions? I am your son. Is there any chance
that I could be your 'friend', or would that be a breach of
protocol? Hang it all, Mother, who makes these rules? I shan't
press the matter, but if you were to 'friend' me, rest assured I'd
confirm your request at the push of a button, not leave you
hanging in the ether like a chump.

> Your son, and soon-to-be 'friend'
> Charles

HRH The Prince William
c/o Buckingham Palace
London   17 November 2010
England

Dear William

So, you're going to make an honest woman of this Kate girl,
eh? (Or should I say 'Catherine'? 'Kate', 'Catherine',
somehow both feel awkward.) Splendid! Your past oats are
sown, the game's up and there we are then, marvellous. Of
course, the whole enterprise has my most cordial blessing. Just
to check, this girl — she's the one, isn't she? You haven't some
other filly in stow, looking on from afar with coltish, longing
eyes or what-not, have you? No? Good! Because you know,
well — you know.

Anyway, my son, as you know these are straitened times and
we must bear this in mind when planning the wedding. Some
Pomp, yes, some Circumstance in moderation, but where can
we show willing to economise?

How about biodegradable paper plates and instead of
champagne, some of my home-brewed prune wine? As for the
wedding dress, my wife Camilla — your stepmother — would be
perfectly willing to 'hand down' one of her party frocks which,
with some alteration, would fit Kate. Also, on the subject:
would you object if I wore my Wellingtons to the wedding? My
valet would have me wear tight black shoes, but they hurt like
blazes after a long day.

> Frugally yours
> 'Dad'

The Royal Household

MEMO TO ALL STAFF

Highgrove
England   3 December 2010

This has been prompted in part by a complaint from my son,
Prince William. It concerns jokes made by Royal personages
and the need for an honest response to them, in order to
prevent later embarrassment.

Some of you may remember being gathered together when
William came down and was kind enough to give a little
informal talk. During the course of that talk, he made the
following off-the-cuff quip concerning his upcoming
involvement in the bid to host the World Cup in 2018:

> 'I know that we can deliver extraordinary public occasions
> and celebrations. I certainly hope so, as I'm planning quite
> a big one myself next year!'

And of course, you all laughed heartily, giving every
indication that you were very amused indeed. It was a dry
reference to his impending marriage. What you may not have
realised is that he was 'running by you' a line he proposed to
use in his actual speech. You encouraged him to put it in, but
when it came to the 'Big Day', I'm afraid to report that it went
down like the proverbial lead balloon. To use a phrase of my
youth, it laid an egg. I am not suggesting this caused us to lose
the bid and I would certainly not put it past the rival Russian
delegation to have fought down their belly laughs at the joke
just to make the English bid look bad and humiliate the Prince.
All the same, if it turns out that you really didn't think the joke
was 'much cop' and were simply trying to humour the Prince,
I'm afraid you did him, and your country, a disservice.

In future, when I or any other member of the Royal Family

makes a joke, we'd be obliged if you could respond to it on its merits. If it makes you laugh, yes, laugh out loud! But if it doesn't, remain stony-faced. That way, we know where we stand. You know I'm open to criticism — you've always said I am when I've asked you. Well, then, hang it all, don't be so bloody deferential! And that's a Royal Command.

Yours, &c
HRH The Prince of Wales

Hoofers, Entertainers and Celebrity Folk

Uri Geller
c/o Parkinson
The British Broadcasting Corporation
London
England   6 April 1974

Dear Mr Geller

If I were King, and this were the twelfth century, I could command you to show me how to do that trick of yours with the spoon and you'd jolly well have to do it or you'd be hanging by your thumbs in the Tower until you did.

Of course, it's not the twelfth century, you're an Israelite and I'm not crowned yet, so I'm going to have to ask you instead. During grace the other day my mother caught me rubbing a soup spoon and shot me a glance that made me feel all of twelve years old and sent to my room to sit on the 'Disgrace Stool'.

Back to my point: I believe in this world there are spiritual forces at work denied by science and the machine age – powerful, invisible vibrations we have not yet learned to harness. With your help, I should like to harness them. Between you and me, I often have dreams of being a 'Wizard King', issuing decrees by directing the forces of nature with just a jab of my forefinger. It seems to me you have those powers. What puzzles me is all you ever seem to do is bend spoons. I mean, hang it all! Here we are with untapped, supernatural forces at our disposal and all we're producing is wonky cutlery. You teach me the trick and I'll supply the vision for Britain – we could do great things.

> Yours, in faith
> HRH The Prince of Wales

Hoofers, Entertainers and Celebrity Folk

Mike Yarwood
c/o The British Broadcasting Corporation
Wood Lane
London
England   12 March 1975

Dear Mr Yarwood

'And this is me' – that's your catch phrase, I believe? Well, this
is *me*: Prince Charles. I say this because it has been known for
my correspondence to be sent back to me on the assumption
that it's some sort of fabrication concocted by a malicious
impersonator.

You, I do not consider a malicious impersonator. As a
family, I should say we have raised a wry smile at your Frank
Spencer, your Brian Clough, your Mr Wilson and various trade
union leaders. And one is flattered to note that one has also
joined the ranks of your hallowed repertoire. An honour indeed!

Might I advance a little constructive criticism, though? I
sometimes look in the mirror as I practise my public speeches
and I have to say, what I see doesn't altogether tally with the
version of one that one sees when one tunes into *The Mike Yarwood
Show*. I don't say this out of any wounded pique but when I see
you doing me, rather than reminding me of me, it reminds me
of Mike Yarwood. Indeed, I think the same could be said of your
Frank Spencer, your Brian Clough, your Mr Wilson and your
trade union leaders. All of them remind me of Mike Yarwood.
When you say, 'and this is me', I need hardly reminding of it.

As I say, constructive criticism. I hope you will take this on
board and that your confidence is not damaged in any long-
term manner.

Affectionately, yours
HRH The Prince of Wales

Harry Secombe
c/o Broadcasting House
London
England   17 May 1977

Dear Mr Secombe

As you know, you've always been one of my favourite
'funnymen' — in times of old, you'd doubtless have capered
about my court in a cap'n'bells and Harlequin's outfit, shaking
a bladder on a stick and making remarks for which I would have
had my Lord Chancellor beheaded, had he dared make them.
None of that in modern times, of course, though one does get
the nagging feeling that in ridding ourselves of the old ways, we
have perhaps lost something.

But back to the point: as an occasional mirth-maker myself
(amateur, but with one or two flattering 'notices' under my
belt!), I'm fascinated by the idea of the 'formula' of comedy. In
your case, I'd say it's as follows:

    30% fat
    25% 'zany' voice
    40% Welsh
    5% 'x-factor'

Is that a fair summary, do you feel? I'm not, of course,
saying there is anything inherently amusing about the Welsh —
I'd get into fearful hot water, were I to say that — just that you
make being Welsh feel very funny indeed. As for that 'x-factor',
what is it, I wonder? Sweat? You do sweat a lot, I've noticed at
close quarters. I hope this is not because you feel ill at ease
among royalty.

        Your old chum
        HRH The Prince of Wales

Morecambe and Wise
c/o BBC Television Centre
London
England   6 January 1978

Dear Eric — or is it Ernie?

Anyway, it's the funny one I wish to talk to, if that aids
identification. I have a question that has been bugging me for
some time — some years, in fact. It concerns your act. Now, I
pride myself on having a tremendous sense of humour, within
the bounds of reason, of course. And I must admit I laugh
myself silly at your antics on the 'Christmas Show' — I am long
accustomed to amusing my brother Edward with that thing you
do with the paper bag.

However, there is one 'bit' that leaves me stone cold: when
you shout the word 'Arsenal' for no reason. 'Arsenal!' you
shout. But I simply don't get it — what am I missing? They seem
a creditable football team, not much better or worse than any
other in the First Division on their day. I was in my rooms at
the Palace the other day and tried it out on myself. 'Arsenal!' I
barked three times at myself in the mirror. I wasn't tickled in
the least. Unfortunately, my sister Anne happened to be
passing along the corridor and looked in, caught me at it and
departed shaking her head, her low opinion of my mental
condition apparently confirmed.

So, why 'Arsenal' — why not 'Manchester United'?

Yours, in earnest curiosity
HRH The Prince of Wales

Eileen Derbyshire (aka Emily Bishop)
Coronation Street
Granada Studios
Manchester
England   15 January 1978

Dear Miss Derbyshire

I wish to pass on my condolences to Emily for the tragic and
brutal death of her husband Ernest on the operating table,
following a shooting on the factory floor.

I am, of course, no 'crank' and fully aware that all this is
made up for television but even so, Emily must be very real to
you and in order to play the role, you yourself must be feeling
deeply for her – as we all do. It has certainly made me think
deeply about crime in the streets: such senselessness, what a
waste of human life. Something really must be done – and
fast – so that no has to go through what you have gone through.

>   With deepest sympathy
>   HRH The Prince of Wales

Eileen Derbyshire
Coronation Street
Granada Studios
Manchester
England   18 March 1979

Dear Miss Derbyshire

I hope you don't think it forward of me to write to you like this,
especially on a delicate and rather personal matter, but
Coronation Street has always been a favourite fixture of the Royal

Household and although it is of course just a regional soap opera, I feel it is embedded in warm, earthy truth. In particular, I feel you could not play Emily Bishop as well as you do, were you not a similar sort of person yourself. It is hard, for instance, to imagine Miss Barbara Windsor (no relation) playing the same role. I particularly admired the way you handled the tragic death of your husband, Ernest.

I wonder then if I might discreetly sound out your advice on my prospects? My uncle, Lord Mountbatten, believes a young man like me should 'play the field', dally with a few game and saucy wenches of good breeding, but liberal inclination before ultimately settling down. Countervailing opinion, however, suggests that I 'keep my powder dry', so to speak, and wait for 'Miss Right'. What would you advise were you my mother? I'd ask my own mother, but somehow I feel more comfortable asking you.

> Hopefully, yours
> HRH The Prince of Wales

The Producer
Coronation Street
Granada Studios
Manchester
England   6 May 1981

Dear Sir

As you know, I'm getting married to the lady who will shortly become Princess of Wales. I'd just as soon there wasn't any fuss but you know, the bloody press, it's all being got up as a fairytale and well, one has to do one's duty to one's people, who have given the King Charleses of the past a bit of a mixed reception.

Here's the thing: my mother and grandmother are both fans of your show as, sporadically, am I (do give my warmest regards to Miss Eileen Derbyshire, or 'Emily Bishop', with whom I have had the pleasure of corresponding frequently), which is how I have come to discover there is a wedding planned between two of the characters — 'Ken' and 'Deirdre' — which will coincide with my own (both televised).

Now there's always the danger that the one could 'crowd' out the other so I was wondering, is there any chance you might put the wedding back a few weeks? I'd hate the dashed humiliation of my own nuptials being overshadowed by a couple of made-up characters. After all, this thing between Diana and me it's very real and if this is reality (and I suppose it is), certainly quite real.

Perhaps the scriptwriters could have 'Ken' postpone the wedding? He might have doubts, you know. A younger woman, a slightly older man, who may perhaps be wiser marrying someone of his own age group, perhaps a long-term, trusted companion . . . Thoughts along those lines could worry 'Ken' and he may suggest they postpone or even declare the whole thing a washout. Yes, it could be for the best. Oblige me, there's a good fellow.

Yours &c
HRH The Prince of Wales

Judith Hann
Tomorrow's World
BBC Television Centre
Wood Lane
London
England   6 January 1983

Dear Miss Hann

This is just to say how terrifically excited I am about appearing on *Tomorrow's World*. It is one of my very favourite television programmes, a marvellous showcase for British know-how and ingenuity, not to mention a fascinating 'sneak peek' into what life will be like in the future, when no doubt my mother will be making her way to the opening of the Houses of Parliament by jetpack!

I can't pretend my wife, Princess Diana, is interested in your show or will even be watching my appearance on it. She doesn't trouble to hide her yawns throughout its duration and frequently glances at her watch. If she had one of the 'time travel' machines, which I expect British boffins are working on right now, she would use it for no other purpose than to travel from 7.00 to 7.30 each Thursday evening so that she could get straight to *Top of the Pops* – a dreadful shame, and we have had words on the subject.

I thought I would take the liberty of 'running by you' two or three inventions of my own, some at the garden shed stage, others still at the drawing board, all of which would need help from experts to realise their full potential as my own time is at a premium.

- The core-less apple: Is there a way of creating one of these things without tampering with the organic processes of nature? I hope so. Cores, quite literally, give me the pip!

- The self-erecting easel: I get so little time to paint and when I do, I end up spending half my time putting up the blasted easel – which, as modern contraptions go, is about as annoyingly counter-intuitive as the deckchair. It would be nice if, when moving from spot to spot, special robot legs could be devised so that the easel could simply up and walk with you, like a sort of caddy or man. I calculate that in the time saved, I might produce at least one more canvas per sitting – a real boon.

- The 3D Three Degrees Simulator: Imagine, you have a yen to see this tremendous singing group in person, but they are out on tour. Simply switch on the Simulator and there the three ladies are, in matching evening dresses and perfect syncopation. 'When Will I See You Again?' Any time you want, at the mere flick of a switch, performing their greatest hits!

I wonder if you might get one or two of your best people to work on these, particularly the last one? Also, establish the feasibility of it running off compost or animal waste?

> Yours, in innovation
> HRH The Prince of Wales

John Travolta
Hollywood
California
United States of America   1 December 1985

Dear Mr Travolta

You may well remember that the other evening, at a smart function, you consented to dance with my bride, Princess Diana. One felt like a lemon sitting on the edge of the dancefloor, knowing if one were to attempt the same steps oneself, one would probably be precipitated base over tip, doubtless taking one's wife down with one and leaving one's dignity in ruins. Meanwhile, one's wife would be staring at one in a smoulderingly reproachful manner and a following day's worth of papers best avoided entirely, despite their element of serious current affairs content.

None of that happened, but I couldn't help but feel on the quiet carriage journey home that my wife was looking at me in a 'Why aren't you John Travolta?' sort of way. I may be entirely mistaken in this, of course. However, it could be that as a result of your dance, she is in her own mind building you up to be quite something.

Could you be a jolly good fellow and write, assuring her perhaps that you're not all you're cracked up to be? That, I don't know, you're a dull conversationalist, or you dislike Duran Duran intensely, or that you mostly spend your days in a potting shed sorting through your collection of clay pipes? Or, if all else fails, that you're homosexual? The future stability of the Monarchy might depend on this kind act.

Expectantly, yours
HRH The Prince of Wales

John Travolta
Hollywood
California
United States of America   18 December 1985

Dear Mr Travolta

Further to our last correspondence, I don't know what you
wrote to my wife but it doesn't appear to have done the trick.
She still looks at me like I've just trodden on her foot in the
middle of the dancefloor. Could you possibly have another
pop, taking a different 'tack'?

> Yours &c.
> HRH The Prince of Wales

Harry 'Loadsamoney' Enfield
c/o Channel 4
Charlotte Street
London
England   12 February 1987

Dear Mr Enfield

Well, I'll get down to brass tacks. While, as a 'Footlights' man, I
appreciate wacky comedy, I cannot but help think that in the
present climate, the flaunting of 'wedge' as you have it might
excite resentment in the regions or rural districts, where
deprivation is at its most fearful.

Could you not reasonably moderate the character? Perhaps
call him Mr 'Quite Well-To-Do, Thank You' and cut out the
flaunting of the banknotes? To compensate for any loss of

humorous 'impact', you might have the character roll his trousers up and paint his knees green, or be called 'Occledooze' — that sort of thing works for Spike Milligan and myself. Or fire yourself out of a cannon and say, 'I'm enjoying this boom!' That is a pun, by the way.

One likes to laugh, but one must think of the inner cities.

Yours, in earnest
HRH The Prince of Wales

Ben Elton
c/o Channel 4
Charlotte Street
London
England   4 June 1987

Dear Mr Elton

So, word reaches me that you are in the frontline of 'alternative' comedians. Well, you'll find in your future monarch a kindred spirit, a man who himself is a great believer in the alternative — therapies, homeopathic remedies, Reiki head massage and the like. Hang it all, we're practically the same, you and me — impatient, wanting to see things get done!

Knowing you are a lover of the humorous, I must pass on an exchange I had with an Impresario at a recent West End function. He had been in touch with Mr Andrew Lloyd Webber, who is in the process of putting together one of his musical extravaganzas. He was looking for someone to write the book — you know, the lyric — and for some reason, your name entered the conversation. To cut a long story short, the misapprehension arose that I had mooted you as a collaborator with him.

How I guffawed! It's been said of me, rudely by family members, that I am apt to advance the most far-fetched and hare-brained suggestions but the very thought of you two fellows in cahoots had our party roaring with laughter, myself loudest of all. Now, back to the real world. Edible exercise books in school . . . Have you given any thought to this matter?

> Yours, indeed
> HRH The Prince of Wales

Lenny Henry
The British Broadcasting Corporation
London
England   18 January 1988

Dear Mr Henry

First of all, I should like to congratulate you on being in all likelihood Britain's foremost black entertainer, breaking down barriers of prejudice and giving us all a much-needed good laugh. I know David Bellamy roars at your impersonation of him – you seem to have a tremendous feel for what white people are like. Which brings me to the matter at hand. It occurs to me, as Heir, that I will be presiding over a number of citizens from the black community. I will be their king as well and as such, I feel duty-bound to get to know them better, inside out.

To this end, I have devised a plan, which I thought I would present to you for your response. I propose, for a few days, to live in the black community disguised as a black man to find out more about how black people live, how they think and feel, in work and at play; observing them at close hand. You know, whenever I meet anyone, they're always on their best

behaviour — it makes me wonder what they would be like if they didn't know it was one.

Of course, I know how badly this could possibly backfire: I might accidentally give myself 'away', which could be exceedingly embarrassing, or too little care could go into the make-up, leaving me like one of those minstrels about whom many of us now feel absolutely awful. Which is why it's important that the make-up job be first rate.

I put the idea to one of my footmen, who it so happens is black, and insofar as it's possible to gauge the reactions of a man suddenly stricken with a coughing fit, he did not appear to disapprove of the idea. Do you?

> Yours, anxiously
> HRH The Prince of Wales

Lenny Henry
The British Broadcasting Corporation
London
England   18 January 1988

Dear Mr Henry

Thank you for your response and yes, as you delicately put it, the whole idea does seem potentially catastrophic on a number of levels. Thanks for your honesty, though I must say one isn't entirely convinced — I so want to 'help'.

> Yours &c
> HRH The Prince of Wales

Jimmy Savile
Leeds General Infirmary
Leeds
Yorkshire
England   6 March 1992

Dear Mr Savile

I don't think I've ever complimented you on the tremendous job
you have done in educating people as to the nuances and details
of the 'rock'n'roll' and 'pop' scenes. 'Ladies and gentlemen, the
one and only Tina Charles', 'Ladies and gentlemen, the one
and only Rod Stewart & The Faces', 'Ladies and gentlemen, the
one and only Abba', 'Ladies and gentlemen, the one and only
Bay City Rollers' . . . One goes away from your radio broadcasts
feeling so much more informed.

   I wonder, therefore, if I might persuade you to help me put
together a cassette tape of pop songs, which I intend to present
to my wife as a birthday present. I want to show her that I'm
'with it' and attuned to modern tastes, but so far all I've been
able to think of putting on it is the one and only Duran Duran,
the one and only Elton John, the one and only Phil Collins and
the three and only Three Degrees.

   You have your ear to the ground, you know the 'scene' –
would you help a fellow out?

          Yours &c
          HRH The Prince of Wales

Hoofers, Entertainers and Celebrity Folk

Julian Clary
c/o Channel 4
Charlotte Street
London
England   18 September 1992

Dear Mr Clary

I am writing to congratulate you on your homosexuality. Not everyone would agree with your right to exist as such, especially among the religious communities of whom I am Defender, but I think in time we can all sit together at the table of reasonableness and thrash out some sort of compromise in plain and simple language – free, one hopes, of the 'double-entendres' that are your stock in trade!

I'm writing to you, as one of the leaders of the homosexual community, on what you understand is a purely hypothetical matter. Suppose one harboured the suspicion – no, strike that, impression – that a member of one's own family were homosexual? What would you advise? Not everyone can 'come out' in the way you did – for a start, you might find yourself out of a job if they did!

To the best of one's knowledge there hasn't been a homosexual in the Royal Family in many centuries, since Edward II, and even then, it might have been dramatic licence on the playwright Marlowe's part. Are we statistically, even genetically, unusual? And if so, what are the odds of the family tree bearing one now? Perhaps we might discuss this matter privately, though still hypothetically, I cannot emphasise enough, at your earliest convenience.

Yours, man to man
HRH The Prince of Wales

The Prince Charles Letters

Julian Clary
c/o Channel 4
Charlotte Street
London
England   22 September 1992

Dear Mr Clary

Regarding my letter the other day, I've given the matter further thought and decided to give the matter no further thought. It is quite unthinkable!

> Yours &c
> HRH The Prince of Wales

Eileen Derbyshire
(aka Emily Bishop)
c/o Granada Studios
Manchester
England   18 January 1994

Dear Miss Derbyshire

Well, for reasons you have doubtless read about my own life has become something of a 'soap opera', as I find myself in a so-called 'love triangle'. I sometimes wish, as with you, that the credits could roll and there might be a day or so respite before it all strikes up again but alas, life is life – a 24-hour a day commitment!

I am sure you have read all about my affairs in the newspapers so I shan't rake over them here. Suffice to say, I do find myself wondering what Emily would have made of it all. I feel you are disappointed in me, Emily, the way you sometimes are in Ken when he goes 'off the rails' — or worse, Mike Baldwin. I suspect Emily might even scold me. Would you? I think I'd find that hard to bear, like a mother's harsh words.

If you could, in Emily's character, find a few words to say to me that you think might be both wise and reassuring at this time, I'd dearly appreciate reading them. If, however, you feel that Emily would be unable to bring herself to comment, perhaps you could get Percy Sugden, your lodger (or the actor who plays him at any rate) to convey to me a similar message to that effect.

> Yours, in eternal confusion
> HRH The Prince of Wales

Noel Edmonds
'Crinkley Bottom'
BBC Television Centre
London
England   6 April 1994

Hello there, Noel!

And no, this isn't one of your hilarious 'spoofs' — this is the actual Prince Charles. You're something of a national institution, you know — from *The Multi-Coloured Swap Shop* to 'Mr Blobby' and the 'House Party', somehow you and your familiar beard sum up England and its mentality.

I have a favour to ask: I'm doing a presentation on eco-sustainability in Lancashire, in the regions. It's an outdoor event and there will be young people there. It would impress them enormously if you were to make an 'impromptu' appearance. I see it mapping out as follows: I begin an address on the need to drastically cut down on our frivolous, wasteful use of fossil fuels. In your helicopter you descend from the skies, land, step out and in a few words endorse everything I've said, adding some comments about the need to conserve oil. Then you step back into your helicopter and with one last wave, fly off. I think it would really drive home 'the' message.

> 'Blobbily' yours!
> HRH The Prince of Wales

Spike Milligan
c/o The British Broadcasting Corporation
Wood Lane
London
England   18 August 1994

Dear Mr Milligan

You can keep your Monty Pythons, your Jim Davidsons, your Harry Enfields and Reg Varneys – much as I remain uncrowned, so too do you – the uncrowned King of Comedy! Your remarks at the microphone show you still have the golden touch when it comes to the funny bone. It wasn't until I saw your film, *Down Among The X Men*, that it occurred to me how much the word 'guerilla' sounds like 'gorilla'. Your comedy enlightens, as well as amuses.

I think it's a crying shame that you are not a permanent fixture nowadays in the light entertainment schedules, although of course in regard to this, it is vitally important that we keep the feelings of both the Irish and Pakistani communities in mind.

At an awards ceremony, you called me a 'grovelling little bastard'. I must confess, when I first got word of this, the blood drained to my boots and I practically swallowed my Adam's apple. Rather stunned I was. Slowly, however, and with careful explanation from a trusted member of staff, I came to realise the remark was meant in a spirit of amusement and I have now taken it on board. In fact, it has become rather a joke with my staff. I say things to them like, 'All right, you grovelling little bastards! I need my septic tank draining promptly,' or, 'See you, grovelling bastard, my shoelaces won't do themselves up, you know!' It's been several days and they haven't tired of it yet. We need humour of your sort in order that we don't get above ourselves.

>Grovellingly yours!
>HRH The Prince of Wales

Billy Connolly
Sydney
Australia   13 January 1995

Dear Billy

Jolly good to have you over the other weekend, 'laddie'! I have a feeling we are destined to become terrific 'pals'. It may well be that some will revile you as a 'toady', particularly those of your countrymen of a Jacobin bent, for consorting with the likes of oneself. Ignore them – they are probably jealous! More than likely, they wish it was they, and not you, who had the privilege of being present at the slideshow presentation of my visit to the National Fruit Board.

Incidentally, I appreciate you were a little tired and had to retire early, two hours into the presentation, but you see, that isn't actually done in one's presence. Has anyone had a word with you? They probably will in due course.

> Your dear chum
> HRH The Prince of Wales

Rory Bremner
c/o Channel 4
Charlotte Street
London
England   17 July 1996

Dear Mr Bremner

I hope you don't think I'm 'taking' a liberty but as one with a 'Footlights' pedigree, I wonder if I might submit for inclusion on your show a sketch written by oneself and rather 'taking the rise' out of oneself? It goes as follows:

> (SCENE: The pantry, Buckingham Palace, in the small
>   hours. It's late at night and PRINCE CHARLES, in a
>   dressing gown, sneaks quietly in and makes straight for
>   the bread bins, opening each in turn. As he does so, HM
>   THE QUEEN, also in a dressing gown, appears at the
>   pantry door.)
> QUEEN: What the devil is one doing?
> CHARLES: I'm looking for a roll.
>
> (Laughter)

The role/roll pun will work better aurally than on paper, I'm confident. It's intended more as a 'rib-tickler' — so much satire is designed to wound nowadays.

Yours, in comedy
HRH The Prince of Wales

Rory Bremner
c/o Channel 4
Charlotte Street
London
England   30 July 1996

Dear Mr Bremner

I'm sure by now you've received, and had a wry chuckle at the sketch I submitted to you the other day. However, I must urge you to stick precisely to the wording and not be tempted to 'improvise' around it. I say this because I decided, by way of a parlour game at our most recent family gathering, to give the sketch a try-out with various members of my family playing the roles. My mother, HM The Queen, played herself but refused to say 'one', instead insisting on 'you' and claiming it was less 'hackneyed'.

Edward played myself, first of all. For a theatre man, my brother was, I'm afraid, hopeless. Not only did he linger a beat coming into the punchline but he delivered it as follows: 'I'm looking for a bread roll.' Needless to say, he missed the sense of the line and I was the recipient of some jolly unjust blank looks.

My sister Anne then took a turn at playing the Queen. This time I played myself without a hitch. However, the lines went as follows:

ANNE (AS QUEEN): What the devil are you doing?
CHARLES (AS CHARLES): What the devil is ONE doing?
I'm looking for a roll!
ANNE (AS QUEEN): Well, that's the only roll you'll be
given around here while I live and breathe.

At which point everyone roared, but you see Anne had missed the point. Mine was the punchline, not that thing she made up. She'd stolen my thunder and in so doing torpedoed the entire sketch.

Finally, I decided to play HM The Queen, if only to get her line right. This time, Prince Philip (my father) played oneself:

CHARLES (AS QUEEN): What the devil is one doing?
PHILIP (AS CHARLES): Well, there are three people in my
marriage and it's a bit overcrowded, so I thought I'd sleep
down here.

Which brought the bally house down, but once again was completely straying from the point of the sketch. Whereupon I abandoned the entire exercise and stormed out. My family have absolutely no sense of comedy.

Yours, in disgust
HRH The Prince of Wales

Michael Caine
Hollywood
California
USA   19 April 2001

Dear Mr Caine

Like me, you're a busy man so I won't detain you long. At
Palace Christmas parties, it's my custom to entertain family
members with a selection of 'impersonations'. They have to
guess who I'm doing. Between you and me, they're not always
very good at doing so.

Last year, I did you . . . and drew a complete blank. So, I'm
going to have another go this year. Just to clarify, is it:

'MOI name is MICHAEL CINE'

'My NIME is MOICHAEL CAINE'

or

'MOI NIME is MOICHEL CINE'?

Really, you'd think mentioning your name in the
impersonation would have been all the help they needed, but
still they professed to be quite stumped, even Anne. I got very
exasperated, which made them all titter . . . which only steamed
me up all the more. Why would they be so obtuse?

> Yours – and 'not a lot of people know that!'
> HRH The Prince of Wales

William Roache
aka Ken Barlow
c/o Granada Studios
Manchester
England   18 April 2005

Dear Mr Roache

I'm not one of those people who thinks soap opera characters
are real-live people – they say I'm out of touch but credit me
with some marbles! That said, with the greatest respect, Ken
Barlow is the person I know and the one I'm really interested
in. You'll understand.

So, if you'll indulge me, I'll address myself to Ken. You,
Ken, strike me as the most reasonable man on television. We
were married around the same time, we have suffered ups and
downs, and often feel like we have never quite found our true
role. Both of us have wrestled with our consciences, like a
couple of 'Mick McManuses'.

I was wondering, Ken, if you could come up to Highgrove
and have a broad, free-ranging discussion about what's to be
done about things. If I could turn back to you, Mr Roache, and
explain what I mean by this. I'd like you to come up to
Highgrove, where you would of course be put up, but for you to
sit down and converse with me in the character of Ken. It is his
views, his counsel I seek. Naturally, you may pitch in as well –
just say, 'And if, Sir, I could just put in a word as William' – but
in the main, Ken's the man I want to hear from.

Earnestly, yours
HRH The Prince of Wales

Bill Oddie
c/o *Autumnwatch*
The British Broadcasting Corporation
London
England   7 April 2006

Dear Mr Oddie

Well, you've come a long way from the days of The Goodies! I
remember guffawing like a drain at your antics back in the
1970s, especially the 'Ecky Thump' episode, to the point where
my sister, HRH The Princess Anne, was quite short with me. 'If
one of my horses was whinnying like that, I'd assume it was in
agony and have the animal destroyed!' she snorted.

As a fellow humorist, I thought I'd share with you quite an
amusing story. In honour of your work at *Autumnwatch*, I
suggested to Camilla that one of the big Nature agencies lobby
for some part of the landscape to be renamed in your honour.
'Sort of, perhaps, Bill Oddie Hill, for example' to which
Camilla replied, 'Sounds a bit like "Bloody hell!" doesn't it?'
On reflection, I had to agree and laughed as if watching a giant
kitten scale the Post Office Tower! Spoken quickly, the results
are unfortunate: Bill Oddie. So, anyway, I'm afraid a hill is out
of the question. Nature and profanity are no bedfellows.

Yours &c
HRH The Prince of Wales

The Prince Charles Letters

Gordon Ramsay
c/o Channel 4 (Cookery Department)
Charlotte Street
London
England   4 June 2007

Dear Mr Ramsay

It's plain from your television series that you wield a fine skillet, a talent I've always admired. I've worn the white hat myself on occasion, though I've always thought I could do with a bit of mentoring in order to bring myself up to scratch.

Which is where you come in. Do you suppose you could spare the time to come up to Highgrove and we could work together amid the pots and pans to really put me through my culinary paces? It would be lovely to surprise Camilla with a Courgette Gratin, just the right side of 'gooey'.

One condition, however. I know you've got a bit of a short fuse so I warn you, I don't respond well to that sort of thing: I get flustered and muddled up. Memories of my father, HRH The Prince Philip, come flooding back – 'NOT LIKE THAT, BOY – GIVE IT HERE, LET ME SHOW YOU FOR THE TENTH TIME! – GOOD GOD, DUMBO! WITH EARS LIKE THAT YOU'D THINK YOU'D BE ABLE TO TAKE IN THE SIMPLEST INSTRUCTIONS – NOW TRY IT AGAIN. NO, NO, NO! YOU'VE MADE A PIG'S RUMP OF THE WHOLE THING! YOU'RE AN IMBECILE, BOY – WHAT ARE YOU? LOUDER, DON'T SNIVEL! THAT'S RIGHT, AN IMBECILE! NOW GET OUT OF MY SIGHT!'

> Yours &c
> HRH The Prince of Wales

Hoofers, Entertainers and Celebrity Folk

Simon Cowell
c/o *The X Factor*
ITV
London
England   2 February 2008

Dear Mr Cowell

First, I must compliment you for I identify with you. To have
persisted these many years with such a singularly unfashionable
haircut shows (as some might say it does in me) a defiance and
quality of mind rare among men. As to your show, *The X Factor*, I
wonder, as one distinctively coiffured modern gentleman to
another, if I could make a request?

You see, I have a footman – actually, I have *two*, one for
both feet (a joke as you've doubtless realised), who fancies
himself as something of a 'crooner' or 'belter'. He does a
rendition of a song entitled 'Wonderwall' by the group Oasis,
which I can only describe as voluble. I shouldn't like to see him
suffer the agonies of audition by television set, might I
therefore suggest you come up to Highgrove and give him the
once-over?

While here, and this is very much an afterthought, I'd like
your opinion on a little act of my own. I shan't give the game
away at this stage but suffice it to say, I doubt there's another act
in Europe who can capably perform 'When Will I See You
Again' by The Three Degrees on a 'pair' of eighteenth-century
basting spoons.

> Yours, in keen anticipation
> HRH The Prince of Wales

Jeremy Clarkson
c/o *Top Gear*
The British Broadcasting Corporation
London
England   12 May 2008

Dear Mr Clarkson

I should begin by saying that I don't think we quite see eye to
eye on this whole global warming business. You think it's a lot
of nonsense got up by the spinach sandal brigade, I say quite
the contrary. And my sandals, I should have you know, are not
made of spinach: they're exclusively hand-stitched by a little
man in the Andorran mountains, durable yet eco-sustainable.
Bury them, and they decompose naturally in the soil, as indeed
did mysteriously happen to three consecutive pairs during the
years with my former wife.

Well, my point is this: under strict conditions, I should like
to come on your television show, *Top Gear*. Not to be a figure of
fun, you must understand – I know what tricks you blighters
can play in the editing suite, which you'd be on your honour
not to play on this occasion. I rather fancy that I could show
your viewers a thing or two about the thrills and spills of eco-
sustainable driving in a vehicle of my own devising, which I call
the 'Poundbury Pelter'.

Picture, if you will, a go-kart-like vehicle with balsa wood
casing and ample room for one man of average-to-above-
average girth. At the rear two recycled cycle wheels, at the front,
a ball similar to the one on the front of a Dyson ball
wheelbarrow. Beneath the seat a small battery engine, which can
run for almost half a mile on a single bucketful of animal dung
(even Mother's corgis have contributed their bit, thanks to my
faithful scoop and the faithful retainer who has the honour of
being its bearer).

The engine is augmented by good old-fashioned pedal power. I fancy that I wouldn't match the sort of times registered by some of your guests in conventional vehicles. Instead of, say, 1m 26s, we'd be looking at more in the order of ten minutes or so. But they'd be ten earth-saving minutes, hang it all, and I'd suggest, absorbing television viewing: we need to slow down the pace of modern life, I feel, not quicken it. Indeed, speaking of gears, I often wish life had a 'reverse gear'. Though I wouldn't care to reverse back to my school years, I'd slam down the brake on the Poundbury Pelter when I approached them (a trowel attached by elastic to some wiring, since you ask).

Talk directly to my people about it — they have my diary.

Yours, in moderation
HRH The Prince of Wales

Jeremy Clarkson
c/o *Top Gear*
The British Broadcasting Corporation
London
England   21 May 2008

Dear Mr Clarkson

I was really most appalled to hear a reference in connection to myself to the 'Poundbury Pelter' on last Sunday's edition of your show. It is one discourtesy not to reply to a man's correspondence, but an altogether bigger one to use its contents to bandy about for comedy purposes on the television set.

I must now withdraw my offer to appear on your show and close this correspondence. It is a shame — the environment will suffer as a result — but there is a principle at stake.

Yours, &c
HRH The Prince of Wales

Al Murray
Al Murray's Happy Hour
c/o ITV Studios
London
England   5 May 2009

Dear Mr Murray

I caught your show on the commercial channel at the recommendation of my father, who described you as 'the only fellow on the gogglebox with enough bloody backside to talk the truth'. I must say, I was deeply affected by your fealty to Queen and Country, and must congratulate you for persisting when all about you were laughing openly in your face.

I regret to say that I know that feeling. Some years ago, I proposed we establish a private bottle bank for my grandmamma, HM The Queen Mother. I meant it earnestly but it was met with a round of guffaws from my family — my Father in particular, who roared, 'Bloody good idea! Recycle her empties and in six months we'd have stitched up your hole in the bloody ozone layer and you'd have to find something else to do with yourself, boy!'

However, touching on the issues you have with the French: persevere. I understand. In 1962, I was forced to take High Tea with the then President de Gaulle on the Palace terrace.

Haughty! There I sat, in an anguish of short trousers and strained silence. Great hairy knees, I thought, if this is the French you can bloomin' well keep 'em. After about an hour he turned stiffly to me and said, 'You 'ave do . . . homeweerrkk?' And I replied, 'Yes, m'sieur.' Not much, I know, but vaguely cordiale. So do persist. I wouldn't exactly say it's worth it, but we must persist.

> A votre (I think that's right)
> HRH The Prince of Wales

Joanna Lumley
c/o The British Broadcasting Corporation
Television Centre
Wood Lane
London
England   19 August 2009

Dear Miss Lumley

We have met before at a Palace function. I vividly recall remarking to you that you looked, 'Absolutely fabulous'. I'd been advised by my wife to avoid saying this because, in her words, 'She probably gets it about half a dozen times a day' but I pressed on anyway and the silvery laugh with which you graced the compliment assured me that my original instincts had been sound.

I must say, I've been most impressed by the way you've 'stuck up' for the Gurkhas in the face of bureaucratic high-handedness and the way you publicly took down that junior Minister a peg or two. I have to admit to a frisson of envy: if I were to be scolded by anyone, Miss Lumley, I should very much like it to be you. I think I would find the experience both stimulating and instructive. Have I been forward? If so, then by all means scold me the next time our paths cross!

>Sincerely, and meaningfully yours
>HRH The Prince of Wales

Michael McIntyre
BBC Television Centre
Wood Lane
London
England   2 September 2009

Dear Mr McIntyre

I make it my business to keep abreast of trends in the light entertainment world and your name came to my attention as 'one to watch'.

In order to assist me in acquainting myself with you, I wonder if you could answer the following questions for my records; questions I suppose anyone might wish to ask of you: who are you and just why are you famous?

>Yours, &c
>HRH The Prince of Wales

Emily Bishop
aka Eileen Derbyshire
Granada Studios
Manchester
England   3 January 2010

Dear Miss Bishop

As the 'Street' enters its sixth decade, you must know that I
think of you as a constant in my life, the sort of person who
would lend a sympathetic ear to a fellow. I know the character
Emily and your late husband Ernest were without issue, so to
speak, but I do regard you as a motherly type.

I wished to provide Emily with some food for thought:
there you are in Lancashire, in the midst of some of the most
magnificent, rolling, rural landscape our country has to offer,
but few, if any, of the plots involve characters outward bound,
taking in the scenery and displacing some of the soot from their
lungs. Instead they're mostly hopping in and out of bed with
one another.

Is there anything you can do about this? Perhaps you and
Ken Barlow could work in league to have a word with the
'powers that be'. I would be happy to provide any backing you
require, lending credibility to your cause.

Yours, always
Charles

Helen Mirren
c/o Equity
Head Office
Guild House
Upper St Martins Lane
London
England   10 January 2010

Dear Miss Mirren

I must say, despite its somewhat poignant subject matter, I greatly enjoyed *The Queen* and thought it largely a success. You yourself got my mother down to a tee – a grand old institution, but a bit distant and not always in tune with modern mores. The fellow who played my father, Prince Philip, was good, too – blunt to a fault, apt to say the wrong thing. And my grandmother: yes, liked a gin. Perfectly observed.

You'll note I said 'largely' a success. May I take issue with the fellow who played myself? He depicts me as a self-absorbed, clipped, ineffectual sort in the chronic throes of some sort of emotional constipation. Well off the mark! It's not a portrait I recognise at all, nor do my staff. Could you bring this up with the actor in question, suggest he might perhaps try some other profession?

　　　　　Yours, &c
　　　　　HRH The Prince of Wales

Hoofers, Entertainers and Celebrity Folk

Tom Cruise
Hollywood
California
United States of America   12 January 2011

Dear Mr Cruise

Well, what with *The King's Speech* and *The Queen*, it's inevitable that at some point they'll get around to making a film about my own life. In which case, I should like to exercise the Royal prerogative and demand you play the role of myself – from the 1990s onwards that is, for my earlier years I should require a younger actor.

As for my wife – Camilla, Duchess of Cornwall – who do you think? Meryl Streep or Glenn Close? I leave the final choice with you, prior to my ultimate approval.

Incidentally, I for one no more believe those absurd rumours of your belonging to the 'Scientology' cult any more than I do the other rumours circulating about you. I mean, spaceships, man – come along now!

> Yours, in eager anticipation
> HRH The Prince of Wales

Colin Firth
Shepperton Studios
London
England   14 February 2011

Dear Mr Firth

I should like to congratulate you, first of all, on your portrait of my late grandfather. I'd be obliged if you could pass on to the filmmakers my appreciation of the discretion they showed in depicting the role of the Royal Family.

Between you and me, Grandmamma wasn't a fraction as fond of Churchill as *The King's Speech* makes out. Indeed, both Grandmamma and my grandfather were squarely behind Halifax, who historians consider a bit of an appeaser. Still, a bit of Vaseline smeared across the historical lens never hurts, especially when it comes to conveying the essential message that the Royal Family are in times of crisis the backbone, heart, soul and conscience of the nation.

In that spirit, and assuming you are currently sniffing around for a 'follow-up', could I press you to take advantage of the current vogue for all things Royal and consider a précis I jotted down yesterday, provisionally entitled *Triumph of a Prince*?:

Set during the Falklands War in 1982, it depicts actual events – a nation plunged into war looks for words of encouragement from the heir to the throne. Margaret Thatcher, a close friend of the Royal Family, urgently seeks his counsel. He, however, is in crisis – unsure of his role, seeking spiritual guidance. This he receives from his mentor Laurens van der Post, and in the final scene, he makes a speech, which although apolitical, rouses the nation and turns the tide of war. A few liberties taken, some might say, but essentially truthful about the King-to-be, the land, its people.

What do you think? I'd suggest you play me, but you are a little old. Would you care for the role of van der Post?

Humbly, yours
HRH The Prince of Wales

Charlie Sheen
Universal Studios
Hollywood
California
USA   2 March 2011

Dear Mr Sheen

I have been perusing some of your recent interviews. It appears you are currently living with two 'prostitutes'. You also state as follows: 'I'm tired of pretending I'm not special. I'm tired of pretending I'm not bitching. I'm tired of pretending I'm not some total [expletive deleted] rock star from Mars.'

It strikes me we have a great deal in common, you and I, we two Charlies. Both sons, so to speak, of our fathers: we are both sceptics about the so-called 'truth', open to the paranormal. I too tire of maintaining the pretence that I am basically none too dissimilar to the 'ordinary chap', even though it is necessary to do so for form's sake. And while I do not regard myself as a 'rock star from Mars', I sometimes wonder if spiritually and perhaps even physically I derive from some higher realm of the cosmos. Like you, I get up a head of steam — gosh, hang it, I am searching for a role because that's how I roll! You roll with me, or I'll roll right over you! I'm Charlie and I'm high on myself. I'm high on Charlie. I'm the KING and I'll melt your faces off!

Unlike you, however, I do try and keep these sentiments 'in check' and I can't say I approve of these prostitutes. Three of you, then — is that not a little overcrowded?

> Yours, really 'kicking backside'
> HRH The Prince of Wales

Sir Bruce Forsyth
Strictly Come Dancing
c/o BBC Television Centre
London
England   13 June 2012

Dear Sir Bruce

'Nice to write to you – to write to you, nice!'

First of all, permit me to congratulate you on your Knighthood. It feels odd, calling you 'Sir Bruce' – like 'Sir Kevin' or 'Sir Gary', somehow it doesn't sit well. But with that thing you do with your fist to your head and so on you've earned it, so that's that. Arise, Sir Bruce! Second, congratulations to you fellows on a terrific television programme – light entertainment at its best, which, were they not watching it, so many people would otherwise be completely wasting their time of a Saturday evening.

To brass tacks, however: I do feel that in laying open the deciding vote to the general public you highlight a grave constitutional danger – that when what my dear, departed grandmother affectionately dubbed 'the teeming, grubby, stinking hordes' are allowed to dictate things through a free vote, they come up with the most frightfully misguided decisions. I mean, John Sergeant, for Heaven's sake? Does this not further highlight the dangers of an elective Republican state in this Kingdom of ours? What I mean to say is, they do keep getting it quite wrong, don't they?

Perhaps in place of the present voting system we could have a committee set up by Royal Appointment, which would have the ultimate casting vote in order to arrive at more sensible decisions? And when this was shown to work well for determining who is chosen as prime minister, you might adopt such a system on *Strictly Come Dancing*.

> Yours, I mean that most sincerely
> (or was that the other fellow?)
> HRH The Prince of Wales

The So-Called 'Fourth Estate': Broadcasters and Their Sort

Kelvin Mackenzie
The Sun
News International
Wapping
London
England   7 April 1988

Dear Mr Mackenzie

I wish to complain about the enormous number of breasts in
your newspaper. Now it's not that I object to breasts *per se* – on
my travels across the Commonwealth I have been 'jiggled' at
more times than you could shake a stick at by bare-breasted
young ladies. This of course is entirely different: those girls
were . . . that's to say, it was entirely anthropological. It was
once considered unthinkable for young women of our own
native land to cavort publicly in that way until your paper
came along.

Of course, you may claim such photographs are 'popular'
with readers, but surely it must concern you that such pictures
erode the calibre of your readership? If you want 'birds' in your
paper, then why not run a series in the page-three slot on the
dwindling numbers of the Dartford Warbler? Now that's 'hot'
news! 'Phwooar!'

> Yours, (I hope) with mutual ornithological fascination
> HRH The Prince of Wales

Chris Evans
c/o Channel 4
Charlotte Street
London
England   5 August 1996

Dear Mr Evans

As you may know, I do look to keep constant surveillance over
the goings-on in the country I am to rule, keeping a weather
eye out for the great and the good, the movers and shakers, the
up-and-the-coming, and what have you. I have noted your
rapid rise to 'DJ' fame and felt it was high time I got to know
you more, to see if there are ways in which we can work together
as we move forward.

I had planned to invite you to Highgrove for one of my
regular soirées, however I seem to have hit a snag and I was
wondering if you were in a position to help me. It seems you
are not liked among certain people. Indeed, you are intensely
disliked. I mentioned your name as a possibility for my
February soirée and within days, received three cancellations.
On hearing you were to come to Highgrove, a member of my
staff bowed her head, then shook it fiercely, and with a
murmured apology, scuttled from the room.

How can this be, I wonder. What is it about you? I'm
deuced if I can see it myself – you seem no different to the
usual, nondescript talking heads one encounters on the
'goggle-box'. If anything, your interviewing style is sycophantic
to a fault. Is it your ginger hair, or your glasses, or perhaps the
celebration of your vast wealth, your nasal, braying manner or
self-obsession? Maybe your treatment of the underlings
featured on your show? Is it that somehow you embody the
acquisitive, greedy, gormlessly materialistic emptiness of
our times?

As I say, this is idle speculation and it would help greatly in my ruminations if you were to sit at your desk and make a list, headed: 'REASONS WHY I AM UNIVERSALLY HATED AND DESPISED'. I must say, should it to be drawn to my attention that I were loathed in the way you appear to be by some people, I would certainly find it helpful to carry out such an exercise myself.

Yours, in assistance
HRH The Prince of Wales

Jeremy Paxman
c/o The British Broadcasting Corporation
Wood Lane
London
England   13 June 2000

Dear Mr Paxman

Reading between the lines, I rather get the impression that like me, you chafe to a large degree at the demeaning trivia of modern life. You yearn for some higher purpose suitable to your abilities and stature; you want to get past the endless round of daily headlines and those humdrum interviews you're forced to conduct with shifty political functionaries and the like. You're casting around for a serious role, a way of really 'leaving your mark'.

Well, perhaps I can help. Following the success, a few years back, of *It's A Royal Knockout*, I was thinking of setting up a similar event to be staged in my gardens at Highgrove – *It's A Royal University Challenge*. I would head up a team of three from Trinity, my old college, while my brother Edward would lead up a team from Jesus. You would be quizmaster. I did give 'first refusal' to Bamber Gascoigne but he rather generously passed on the opportunity, saying you would be far more suitable for the task.

I've already got a team of local carpenters working on a facsimile of the *University Challenge* set. As on the television, there will be an upper and lower deck. I have 'first dibs' on the upper (I always preferred the top bunk bed at boarding school – fellows couldn't drop things on to your face as you slept – spiders, worms, live rats) and the preference remains life-long. I'm having a stepladder installed on the side to help me get up and down – not so limber as I used to be!

I'll leave you to set the questions. You know my specialities – van der Post, The Goons, horticulture, which I trust will be well represented. Quite honestly, I'm hoping to 'wipe the floor' with young Eddie! He doesn't always afford to an older brother the respect that one deserves; he needs whittling down to size in a straight Battle of the Intellects. No favours, but all I urge is that with me, you don't go in for any of that 'C'mon, c'mon, hurry along now!' stuff. It flusters me and I'd be liable to 'dry up', even when the answer's on the tip of my 'tongue'.

One of my staff will let you know which dates we have available.

Yours, finger on the buzzer
HRH The Prince of Wales

Jeremy Paxman
c/o The British Broadcasting Corporation
Wood Lane
London
England   16 June 2000

Dear Mr Paxman

I still haven't received a response to my letter of the 13th. I really am going to have to push you for an answer, you know.

> Yours, &c
> HRH The Prince of Wales

Jeremy Paxman
c/o The British Broadcasting Corporation
Wood Lane
London
England   20 June 2000

Dear Mr Paxman

Still no straight answer, man! Why the evasiveness? Did you receive a copy of my letter? Did you receive a copy of my letter?

> Yours &c
> HRH The Prince of Wales

The So-Called 'Fourth Estate'

Jeremy Paxman
c/o The British Broadcasting Corporation
Wood Lane
London
England   23 June 2000

Dear Mr Paxman

Did you receive a copy of my letter? Did you receive a copy of
my letter? Did you receive a copy of my letter? Did you receive
a copy of my letter? Did you receive a copy of my letter? Did
you receive a copy of my letter? Did you receive a copy of my
letter? Did you receive a copy of my letter?

     HRH The Prince of Wales

Jeremy Paxman
c/o The British Broadcasting Corporation
Wood Lane
London
England   24 June 2000

Dear Mr Paxman

Did you receive a copy of my letter? Did you receive a copy of my
letter? Did you receive a copy of my letter? Did you receive a copy
of my letter? Did you receive a copy of my letter? Did you receive
a copy of my letter? Did you receive a copy of my letter? Did you
receive a copy of my letter? Did you receive a copy of my letter?
Did you receive a copy of my letter? Did you receive a copy of my
letter? Did you receive a copy of my letter? Did you receive a copy
of my letter? Did you receive a copy of my letter? Did you receive
a copy of my letter? Did you receive a copy of my letter?

     HRH The Prince of Wales

Jeremy Paxman
c/o The British Broadcasting Corporation
Wood Lane
London
England   26 June 2000

Well, Paxman
    You may consider this correspondence closed! Stephen Fry
has agreed to step 'into' the breach in your place.

>   Yours &c
>   HRH The Prince of Wales

Michael Parkinson
ITV Studios
London
England   8 January 2001

Dear Mr Parkinson

As a blunt Northerner, you'll appreciate my not 'beating abaht
tha' bush' and getting straight to the point. I like your
interviews, Mr Parkinson. You've interviewed all the greats; you
let your guests TALK, hang it all, rather than upstage them!
Who can forget the time you had Rex Harrison on and he told
an anecdote, some twenty minutes in length, about an adoring
old lady pleading for his autograph at some Hollywood
function, with him finally relenting and then her saying, 'Oh,
thank you so much! I've always been such a big fan of yours, MR
NIVEN!'
    How we roared – all the more a month later when you had
on David Niven and he told a wonderful, lengthy story about

being accosted by some elderly lady outside his club, who asked for his autograph. He finally gave it her and she said, 'Oh, thank you so much! I've always been such a big fan of yours, MR HARRISON!' I'm fond of telling both those stories to my staff. However often they hear them, they always laugh heartily.

Yours, indeed, was the golden age of television and I should like to be interviewed by you now that you have made a comeback. One 'condition', however: often, with your guests, you spring a surprise on them, asking them to do a tap-dancing routine with Sammy Davis Jr, or sing a duet with Miss Kate Bush. I can neither tap-dance nor hold a note. If you were to ask me to do any impromptu 'turn', I'm afraid I'd be forced to decline and your show would have to run to credits early, with ITV controllers having to slot in a 'Potters' Wheel' interlude or public information film before the news bulletin.

Regretfully, yours
HRH The Prince of Wales

The Producers
Big Brother
Channel 4
Charlotte Street
London
England   15 May 2004

Dear Sirs

I must admit to being morbidly drawn to your television series, which does seem to have 'struck' a chord with the general public. It is important we connect, don't you feel, which is why I've been mulling over the idea of a *Royal Big Brother*, with any

monies raised going to a deserving cause such as the
Gooseberry Preservation Society or the League for the Arrest
of the Decline of the Lesser Kestrel.

I'd be game — I fancy my chances of going all the 'way'. Of
course, Mother would probably decline to be involved. Not
sure Anne would be very keen either. As for my father — well,
that's out of the question, of course. The idea of him padding
dozily to the latrine in the small hours amid the green glow of
the night vision camera in just his combinations . . . Camilla is
not, as yet, 'family' as such. So, that would leave myself,
Andrew and Edward, perhaps an unfortunate combination — we
might be inclined to bicker, unsupervised by the maternal eye.

I suppose we could have a *Royal Big Brother* with just members
of my staff and me? I'm afraid there would be very little
acrimony. My staff tend to be very supportive of absolutely
everything I say and do, which is gratifying. Failing all this,
perhaps we could recast the series altogether, instead making it
a celebration of the 'big brother' as a family institution? As a
'big brother' myself, I feel we get rather a raw deal and with
your clout, I'm sure we could turn that around. No need for a
name change, that's the great thing. Just change the contents,
that's all — the details, I leave with you.

Helpfully, yours
HRH The Prince of Wales

Richard and Judy
c/o Channel 4
Charlotte Street
London
England   12 March 2006

Dear Richard and Judy

I must congratulate you both on your career success. Judy, you must feel proud to be an inspiration to older women everywhere. In fact, looking at the pair of you together, I'm often reminded of Camilla and me. Yes, there is a disparity in age and in you, Richard, a certain eternal youthfulness, which some have observed in myself, but there is a bond between you, dammit!

I do catch your show on those occasions when I find myself idle. I trust you'll take the intended compliment when I say that, when I do find myself watching you on TV, it spurs me on to do something. 'There must be something I could be doing,' I find myself saying, and I switch off the television set then go and bally well do it! I believe a great many people up and down the country feel the same way. In this respect, you perform a jolly important function.

> Your admirer, and very occasional viewer
> HRH The Prince of Wales

Fiona Bruce
c/o The British Broadcasting Corporation
Wood Lane
London
England   15 May 2006

Dear Miss(?) Bruce

As one who remembers the news being presented on television
by the likes of Robert Dougall and Peter Snow, may I say what a
welcome fragrance you bring to our airwaves. It was bad enough
in the old days hearing the news about strikes, plane crashes,
three-day weeks, IRA atrocities and butter mountains in the
Common Market without it being read out by fellows who
looked like elderly bloodhounds confined to their kennels on
a rainy day.

   You bring something fresh and new and stimulating to our
channels. I think it's the eyebrows. Sometimes I find it hard to
take in the stories you're reading out — I'm simply watching
your eyebrows levering up and down like drawbridges. How do
you do that? You must come down to Highgrove and show me
some time.

   That was it, really — oh, and despite what you say on
Crimewatch, do take care! We lost Jill Dando, we don't want to
lose you as well.

              Respectfully, yours
              HRH The Prince of Wales

The Editor
News of the World
News International
Wapping
London
England   8 November 2010

Dear Sir

I must admit that I am quite wobbly with alarm to read about this phone-tapping business that appears to be rife among those who find themselves thrust into the upper circles of public life. I mean to say, hang it all, I've had this sort of thing before you know, between myself and my wife, Mrs Parker Bowles and I must admit, the old capillaries boiled with shame when it all came out in the press.

On the one hand it really is, you know, an infringement of liberties – the civil ones that I daresay we all have 'written down' somewhere. On the other . . . well, in a way it would be nice to know one is being bugged. It shows one is important, that one has a vital, key role to play. Not being bugged – well, it suggests the opposite, really – that one's words and thoughts are of no public interest whatsoever. Chastening thought.

So, here's my question to you, fellow to fellow: am I being bugged? If so, what the devil do you think you're doing? Or am I not being bugged? And if not, why not?

Yours &c
HRH The Prince of Wales

The Prince Charles Letters

David Dimbleby
c/o The British Broadcasting Corporation
Wood Lane
London
England   13 December 2010

Dear Mr Dimbleby

I plan to make a special appearance on the BBC to highlight
awareness of my latest initiative, as set out in my recently
published book, *Harmony*. I wish to expound my views on this
important subject on the national channel. Of course, what
with the impending Royal Wedding, I daresay there will be an
appetite for tattle and prattle regarding the ceremony and so
forth, and I suppose, on a quid quo pro basis, I can provide a
few choice 'quotes' to satisfy the national appetite for trivia, to
'sugar the pill' of the main business of the interview, which
would be to provide spiritual uplift.

    I would like the interview to be handled by a seasoned, BBC
man, one who is steeped in the best traditions of the
Corporation, a familiar voice in momentous times over the
decades; one who has gravitas but is not considered 'stuffy', one
in whom an openness to new ideas plus a healthy, inquisitorial
scepticism are perfectly matched.

    You have worked at the BBC for a long, long time. Who do
you suggest? I was thinking Jeremy Paxman or perhaps the 'up-
and-coming' Jeremy Vine. Or, there is Peter Sissons – still a
BBC man? A shame Sir Robin Day is no longer with us, really.

        Yours, in appreciation
        HRH The Prince of Wales

The So-Called 'Fourth Estate'

Andrew Marr
c/o The British Broadcasting Corporation
Wood Lane
London
England   28 May 2011

Dear Mr Marr

I heard a joke the other day: 'What have Prince Charles and
Andrew Marr got in common?'

The answer: 'They're both good listeners.'

Actually, written down like that, I'm not sure that's how the
joke went – I may have misremembered it. Anyway, that was
merely a light-hearted introduction. The meat of my
correspondence concerns these revelations about your private
life. Clearly you've done something of some nature with
somebody or other and funny thing is, I find myself absolutely
riveted. I'm dying to know what it was that you did, who you did
it with and all the whats, whys and wherefores appertaining to
it. This thing, this thing you did – was it really so frightful that
not only can you not mention it, but the highest law makers in
the land decreed no one else must even mention that thing, or
that there was ever any suggestion the thing happened in the
first place, that the thing was ever a thing at all, so to speak?
Least of all mention to whom it was done or whatever the thing
was.

You're torturing a fellow! Can't you 'spill the beans' by
return of correspondence, put me out of my misery? My
imagination is running wild, I can tell you. I have seen things,
you know – in the Navy, on shore leave in some of the former
colonies. I'd hate to think your thing was any of those things.

　　　　　Ravenously, yours
　　　　　HRH The Prince of Wales

Andrew Marr
c/o The British Broadcasting Corporation
Wood Lane
London
England   29 May 2011

'They're all ears!' Yes, that was it . . . Now how about that
unspeakable thing?

      Yours, &c
      HRH The Prince of Wales

Andrew Marr
c/o The British Broadcasting Corporation
Wood Lane
London
England   3 June 2011

Dear Mr Marr

Due to some Post Office bungle, a letter I sent you on 28 May
has been 'Returned to Sender'. This must make the letter I
sent you on 29 May, which I assume you did receive, read
somewhat bizarrely. I'd explain the whole thing again but it's
perhaps best we observe some sort of 'superinjunction'
between ourselves to prevent either of us mentioning this
correspondence ever took place.

      Yours &c
      HRH The Prince of Wales

The So-Called 'Fourth Estate'

Rupert Murdoch
c/o News International
Wapping
London   11 July 2011

Dear Mr Murdoch,

Some months ago, I wrote to one of your editors, asking to know if I had been bugged. Since then, I, along with the rest of the country, would appear to have the answer to this, and a lot of other things besides.

I have gathered my thoughts on this subject, and they are as follows:

You bastards. You ruthless, sociopathic, invasive, utterly indecent, barely human bastards.

Of course, there is an ongoing inquiry into what you people have been up to. If it should turn out that you are entirely innocent, then I cheerfully withdraw in advance the suggestion that you are ruthless, sociopathic, invasive, utterly indecent, barely human bastards.

> Yours &c
> HRH The Prince of Wales

PS It may be that by the time this letter reaches its destination, News International has been 'shut down'. In which case, could I ask the janitor, or whoever is looking after the building, to forward this address in the fullness of time to whichever address, or institution, Mr Murdoch is residing?

Parliamentarians:
Matters of Great Concern

The Prince Charles Letters

George Thomas
Secretary of State for Wales
House of Commons
London
England   6 August 1968

Dear Mr Thomas

I must say I'm terrifically excited about next year's investiture,
which I understand is to be screened on the television set. I
hope I don't go bright red with embarrassment! But I did read
that not everyone's happy about it – these people from the Free
Wales Army, for instance. Actually, I can understand – if some
young 'Taffy' came over to one of our castles and was crowned
the Prince of England, I think I'd consider it a bit thick myself!

All the same, they do sound like a bunch of loonies. Gosh, I
can't repeat what my father said about them! I wonder if there's
anything we can do to prevent hordes of angry Welshmen in red
face-paint charging in over the hills and disrupting the whole
day? Perhaps we could hold the ceremony in England – at, say,
Leeds Castle? Or maybe I could be declared 'Prince of
England, Scotland, Ireland and Wales and The Isles of Wight
and Man' – bit of a mouthful, but then no one feels left out –
except the Orkneys and Lundy whom I forget to put in, like a
chump!

I want to do my best for the Welsh: they haven't got much
going for them apart from the singing, slate mines and rugger,
and I was hoping my investiture would cheer them up a bit,
make them feel they're just as important as everyone else.

Charles (Prince of Wales Elect)

Parliamentarians

The Ministry of Agriculture & Fisheries
House of Commons
London
England   16 August 1969

Dear Sir

I am writing to you regarding over-fishing in the Atlantic. Like
many young people my age, I really am most concerned.

Like anyone else, I enjoy a spot of 'fishing' – to be alone
with nature and a few staff is one of life's great pleasures.
However, when such fishing is undertaken commercially, a
problem arises: the seas are rapidly emptying of these creatures,
I am informed. There simply aren't enough to go round. I'm
terribly worried that at the current rate of consumption by the
year 1980 (by which time I may well have ascended to the
throne of England), the supply of fish will have given out
entirely around these shores.

There must be something that can be done about this. I'm
no politician, but a down-to-earth man interested in practical
solutions. Perhaps the commercial fishermen could be issued
with smaller nets? Or they could use larger nets but with bigger
holes, so that more of the fish fall through them and escape?
Or we could launch a national 'Adopt A Haddock' scheme, in
which selected fish were named, tagged and their seafaring
progress filmed in documentary form by squadrons of 'Jacques
Cousteau'-style frogmen and the results shown on television?
The documentary treatment worked well for the Royal Family –
people were far more disinclined to hunt us down and kill us
once they'd seen us at first hand. Would it not be the same for
the fish?

Charles ('Defender of the Fish')

Arthur Scargill
National Union of Mineworkers
Barnsley
South Yorkshire
England   20 June 1984

Dear Mr Scargill

Well, I'm afraid neither Mother nor my grandmother are
especially fond of you at this moment and if they knew I was
writing to you, they'd probably blow their tops – Grandmamma
especially, who when your name is mentioned, is apt to resort
to the language of the hunt. That's why I'm currently lying
'doggo' in my Palace study as I write this.

But hang it all, in a situation like this it behoves sensible
men to put their heads together and see if a solution can be
reached! I'm no politician but it does seem to me that your
men have been treated in a high-handed manner and I have
spoken about this to Mr Thatcher (Mrs Thatcher's husband) in
the hope that he can put in an influential word. That said, have
you not asked yourself whether mining is really any sort of way
for the human animal to spend his lifespan?

To put it in language you'll understand, 'there's more than
one way to make a muckle'. What I mean to say is, if the mines
have to close, well, perhaps that's a blessing for the
environment – and what's more, an opportunity for your
members to explore more natural, spiritual forms of energy.
I'm talking about chi, ley lines, healing crystals. If they were to
decide to transfer to these areas, I myself could certainly
provide small grants on a first-come, first-served basis to those
of your men willing to wipe the soot from their eyes and see the
world for what it is in the New Age.

Yours, in the spirit of Aquarius
HRH The Prince of Wales

Parliamentarians

The Minister for Architecture
House of Commons
London
England   16 January 1986

Dear Sir

Forgive me for not knowing precisely who you are but with
respect, that is not of the greatest importance. The matter I'm
touching on is far too important for me to be overly concerned
with niceties.

There are a great many of us plain-thinking people who
sit in the back of our cars as we trundle reluctantly through
the capital city and wonder just who on earth built and
commissioned these enormous great slate-grey eyesores,
which dominate the London skyline, like so many vertical
Bulgarias. The people of Britain are not dead-eyed, robotic
rabbits to be herded in and out of dismally lit, polystyrene-
ceilinged, strip-lit cubicles. They are not automatons, they
are subjects and since no one else will speak out, then it must
fall to me.

The soul of England is not rectangular, the spirit of
England is not functional, the mettle of England is not
stainless steel – indeed this whole 'modernist' trend has gone a
jolly sight too far. I sometimes wonder if I bang on about this
sort of thing too much but my staff who are not afraid to
contradict me tell me I do not – so there it is.

Now I am not decrying the twentieth century as a whole.
There have been certain advantages, I will concede: dentistry,
The Three Degrees and I daresay one or two others. But hang it
all, we've become so infatuated with our gadgets, our washing
machines, our microwaving ovens that hang it all, we've lost
touch with nature: the trees, the hedgerows, the marshes and

thickets, what have you . . . the stuff of a vanished, merrier, cement-less golden age. Can we not have both Three Degrees and Thickets?

> Yours, in harmony with Nature
> HRH The Prince of Wales

The Culture Secretary
House of Commons
London
England   22 January 1987

Dear Sir

See here, I wonder if you or one of your top people could help me with something that's been nagging me for days? It's this tune that's been running through my head. I've obviously picked it up from the transistor radio or television set. Goes something like this:

Dum-dum, dum-dum, DE-dum, dee-dee, de—dum . . . tarara dum-dum, de-dum . . . de DUM DUM (big push, there), dum-dum, dum-dum.

One of my staff suggested perhaps it was from something called 'Shake'n'Vac'. Is it, do you think? I'd ask my wife but well, she just rolls her eyes and retreats to the latrine whenever I ask a civil question. I've had my staff working on it for a week now, but really they have far more important things to do, so I was hoping to offload this one on you. There must still be people from Bletchley – you know, those code-breaker johnnies – on the books. Perhaps you could contact your equal at the MOD and check?

No rush, but it you could get back to me — say, this time tomorrow — you'd have no idea of the service you'd be doing your future king.

> Yours, maddened
> HRH The Prince of Wales

The Culture Secretary
House of Commons
London
England   23 January 1987

Dear Sir

Still not heard back from you regarding this tune. Bureaucratic backlog, I suppose — something must be done about that. It's still buzzing around in my head and bugging me like the Dickens.

In order to move forward with this, I'll be dispatching one of my staff down to the Commons to call in at your office in person after she's finished here. I'll brief her by humming the tune to her and she will hum it to you, then we can go ahead on that basis and resolve this once and for all. If you could arrange that she gets the necessary clearance, I'd be most grateful.

> Yours, no less maddened
> HRH The Prince of Wales

Nicholas Edwards
Secretary of State for Wales
House of Commons
London
England   22 February 1989

Dear Mr Edwards

What with its slate mines, singing, hills, striking rain-gauge
readings and vales, Wales really is most terribly interesting. But
it seems Wales has got down at heel. As its prince, I feel a
responsibility to buck it up a bit. Hang it all, something has to
be done otherwise it's in danger of bringing up the rear among
the Home Nations, sort of shambling along with a rope around
its neck.

So, how are we going to bring Wales up to scratch? I've
jotted down a few ideas:

- The language: I've had a stab at it, but it's quite fiendish. I
  suggest we simply get rid of, say, 30% of the consonants and
  replace them with vowels. Which consonants and vowels in
  particular and whereabouts you swap them around, I'll leave
  to you to sort out.

- The coal mines: Let's reopen a few but none of your new
  technology. Let's get back to the days of steam power,
  ventilation furnaces, pit ponies, pick axes, canaries – closer to
  nature. Yes, it was dangerous, but how much more dangerous
  to lose your national soul, dammit?

- The rarebit: Is this an animal? Perhaps you could check,
  because if it is, I suspect its stocks are dwindling faster than
  those of the Dartford Warbler.

- Singing: Welsh people don't sing as often as they used to, in my
  experience. What can be done to correct this?

Yours, in Welshness
HRH The Prince of Wales

John Prescott
House of Commons
London
England   20 February 1998

Dear Mr Prescott

I'd like you to offer my apologies once again for mistaking you for one of my catering staff — a lot of the fellows who work in this capacity hail from northern climes, this being the source of my blunder. I've done it before, I know, and I shall doubtless do it again, but this makes it no less regrettable.

I must commend you, while I have your ear, for the terrific work you're doing in the regions. In the hurly burly of modern life we rather tend to take places like Grimsby for granted, but there's never any chance of that when the likes of you are 'in the chair'. I listen to you and at once I think to myself, 'Grimsby'. For this, and for having ascended from such humble origins, you must be 'reet proud' of yourself, old chap!

　　　　Yours, in (non-political) comradeship
　　　　HRH The Prince of Wales

Stephen Byers
Secretary of State for Trade and Industry
House of Commons
London
England   30 December 1999

Dear Mr Byers

Well, the new Millennium is almost upon us and if many of
the newspapers are to believed, a certain poetic justice is
about to be served in that the vast banks of computers which
shore up our modern lifestyle are about to plunge us back
into the year 1900. Fascinating . . . H.G. Wells couldn't have
made it up.

I have taken my own precautions. In secret, I have had
several of my best men working round the clock to dig me an
underground shelter on my grounds at Highgrove, lined
with aluminium and stocked with tinned foods, utensils,
changes of clothes and even a makeshift convenience. It is
there that I propose to 'sit out' the chaos likely to ensue the
moment Big Ben strikes twelve. I have extended an open
invitation to my family to join me, but they have simply
issued me with what in effect amounts to the 'raspberry'.
And so, it will be just myself, alone, and four members of
my staff (Mrs Camilla Parker Bowles has an invitation to
join me, too).

Upon re-emerging, it may well be that life as we know it has
been utterly transformed, and not necessarily for the worse.
This computer glitch will have catapulted us back to a fairer,
less industrialised era, in which men are closer to the soil.
Society may have to be re-thought, rebuilt from the bottom up,
from scratch. Of course, it will be agreed that the first thing we
will need is a monarchy, which is why I'm going to such lengths
to ensure my own self-preservation. It may be that I am one of

the last men of the old world still standing, but the human cornerstone of a coming New Age. I find that I am strangely calm, all things considered.

> Yours, as New Dawn breaks
> HRH The Prince of Wales

The Secretary of State for Education
House of Commons
London
England   16 October 2000

Dear whoever you are (I apologise – I've been gardening, not had time to check).

Recently there's been a lot of talk about expanding the number of places available to our young people in higher education. On the face of it, this all seems well and laudable but when we dig a little deeper – as I have been this morning – is it really what my old second-form master at Gordonstoun would have described as the 'desideratum'? Aren't there too many people going to university? They're talking about 50% of all young people – is that not rather high?

I suppose it piques me because I'm rather proud of the fact that I went to Cambridge and attained a degree, as did my brother Edward – two from the same family is quite some achievement, particularly in this 'meritocratic' age. I feel my achievement is being cheapened, however, when in this day and age any Tom, Dick or Darren can stroll into one of our major seats of learning and acquire some spurious degree in 'Media Studies' – hang it all, in my day that meant reading the *Beano*!

Could not these youngsters instead take up work in areas such as agriculture, which I feel is much ignored? Get back to the land, learn how to thatch a cottage or twine a haystack, the sort of vital skills that will be key if we are to move forward into the twenty-first century — the countryside? Perhaps these young people could find, and in time, know their place there?

>Yours
>HRH The Prince of Wales (Oxon)

John Prescott
House of Commons
London
England   12 January 2001

Prescott,

Can I distract you momentarily from the Affairs of State and ask you to settle a wager? Is it possible for a man to have a Yorkshire accent and yet not be a socialist? Do please get back to me as soon as possible, as five pounds is riding on this.

>Yours, in urgency
>HRH The Prince of Wales

John Prescott
House of Commons
London
England   18 May 2001

First, you have a bucket of water thrown over you by members of some 'punk rock' group at a pop music awards ceremony. Then you find yourself pelted with eggs by some beefy rustic type in

the shires and you respond with your fists in a pugnacious, if not entirely ministerial manner.

As Shakespeare wrote: 'There's a divinity that shapes our ends, rough-hew them how we will'. I wonder if there's a divinity that shapes your particular rough-hewn ends? I mean, it seems as if you're fated to suffer these episodes. They never seem to happen to Blair, or Harman, or Straw – or the rest of your brigade. Do you think in some way God himself has a hand in these incidents, that they are part of a larger plan in the scheme of which you are, not to be disrespectful, nought but a lump of rude clay to be flung to whatever fate the Deity requires of you?

These are deep thoughts, I agree. I trust they are of help to you as you nurse your bruised knuckles and irritably wave away the press cuttings brought in by your private secretary for your attention.

> Yours, in sympathy
> HRH The Prince of Wales

John Prescott
House of Commons
London
England   21 May 2001

I don't seem to have received a reply to the letter I sent you two days ago. I expect you're busy on the campaign, but just to let you know, the question enclosed in my letter wasn't intended as a 'rhetorical' one. It did require an answer. I'd be grateful to have your response at any time that suits you within the next seventy-two hours.

> HRH The Prince of Wales

Jonathon Porritt
Friends of the Earth
26–28 Underwood Street
London
England   28 January 2002

Porritt,

I hate to tear you away from your vital work but I must tell you
about a dream I had. I was yomping through open fields with a
couple of hounds when I found a clearing and came upon a
large assembly of people. And would you know it, each last one
of them was holding a length of string and attached to those
lengths of string were inflatable effigies of myself. I don't know
what they were doing – unfortunately, my man chose that
moment to wake me up. What can it mean?

Inflatable Prince Charleses! Perhaps the dream was some
sort of message from the untapped, subconscious realm of the
mind, where things make more sense than can possibly be
grasped intellectually. On that basis I'm having a few dozen
commissioned – life-size, as in the dream, and kilted; durable
but biodegradable material, naturally. Question is, what's to be
done with them? They'll be there, but what good purpose can
they serve? Any thoughts? It all feels like a metaphor for
something or other, but I can't think what.

Fraternally, yours
HRH The Prince of Wales

Jonathon Porritt
Friends of the Earth
26–28 Underwood Street
London
England   8 February 2002

If you've had any of the FoE staff working on this inflatable
Charleses idea, stand them down! The things have just come in.
Looking at them, I think the manufacturers have mistaken me
for the late Tony Hancock. They're going straight in the
incinerator.

    HRH The Prince of Wales

John Prescott
House of Commons
London
England   12 July 2002

Could I pick your brains for a moment? I'm venturing up to
the North to speak at a conference on urban regeneration.
Inevitably, there will be Northerners in attendance. I always
make a point, as the Sikh community is aware, of greeting those
groups who reflect the wonderful diversity of Great Britain in a
manner familiar to them, so help me out here. Which of the
following are acceptable because I'm sure I've imagined at least
one of them:

    'A'reet?'
    'Ay up!'
    'Na' then!'
    'Nobbut!'
    'Cock!'

If you could put ticks and crosses in red pen, please, next to each, it'd make for a splendid 'aide memoire'.

> Yours, 'ba'tat'
> HRH The Prince of Wales

John Prescott
House of Commons
London
England   8 August 2002

Well, Prescott

I read they're calling you 'Two Jags' on account of you owning two cars. I suppose, if a man is to be nicknamed thus, then they should be calling me Prince 'Three Jeeps, A Mercedes, Two Bentleys, One Private Plane, One Yacht' Charles. But they don't, you see. Why is that, I wonder? Why is it funny that you own two Jaguars? Is it because it's commonly assumed that a fellow who speaks like you should consider himself lucky to own a bicycle? I'm not making fun of you (I know you are sensitive about that), I am sincerely musing on the irony of life.

I enjoy our correspondence. It is good that we can chat like this, as 'equals'.

> Yours, really most sincerely
> HRH The Prince of Wales

John Prescott
House of Commons
London
England   19 March 2003

It always dismays me when satirists and politicians lambast you for your occasionally mangled syntax. They forget you have travelled further up the social scale to high office than they themselves and your mistakes are to be expected. May I offer a useful 'rejoinder' next time this happens? It's adapted from the comedy duo Morecambe and Wise in a sketch they did with André Previn, a famous conductor. When they accuse you of talking nonsense, tell them, 'I'm saying all the right words – but not necessarily in the right order'. I think you'd hear very little from the 'scoffers' after this!

>   Helpfully, yours
>   HRH The Prince of Wales

John Prescott
House of Commons
London
England   20 March 2003

Something that's always puzzled me about Yorkshiremen – considering their aversion to aitches, a remarkable number of the county's place-names begin with the letter: Huddersfield, Hebden Bridge, Halifax, Hull, Harrogate, Holbeck, Holmfirth, Heckmondwicke, and many, many more. Were these names by any chance imposed by one's Norman ancestors, deliberately intended as ''umiliating' to their alphabetically defective Northern inferiors and intended to keep them in their 'place' as they tried vainly to pronounce them? Perhaps you could look into the matter.

> Yours, inquisitively
> HRH The Prince of Wales

David Blunkett
Home Secretary
House of Commons
London
England   16 April 2003

Dear Mr Blunkett

It seems to me that fellows in my position, the 'haves', bear a duty to the 'have nots' to give something back. In this spirit, I have a large, rusty old septic tank on my grounds. It strikes me that with a bit of elbow grease, application and 'can do' spirit, it could be converted into a small-but-handy, inner-city outdoor swimming pool.

Do please have someone send round a few lads from a socially deprived area with time on their hands and a lorry to fetch the thing. It would clear both my conscience and a bit of space on my grounds.

> Yours, against disadvantage
> HRH The Prince of Wales

John Prescott
House of Commons
London
England   28 April 2006

Dear Mr Prescott

I must say, I rather enjoy our weekly correspondences – on my part, at any rate. It's a shame that the affairs of the day, as you go about doing whatever it is that you actually do, prevent you from answering my letters as often as you would like, if at all.

It pains me to know that you are currently suffering difficulties in what my Uncle Dickie used to call the 'rumpers-pumpers department'. I do miss Dickie. Whenever I reflect upon him, I always dryly remark, much as Mrs Thatcher said of Mr Whitelaw, that every prime minister needs a Willie, so every prince needs a Lord Mountbatten.

I have spoken before about the longings that can beset men of office, of action. We have appetites, which for decency's sake, we must suppress. In the throes of such longings, I take various courses of action. First, open a window. Sometimes a simple act of ventilation does the trick. Second, conjure up a visual memory of the late Israeli prime minister Golda Meir. If that doesn't work, here is a method my father taught me: submit to bee stings. A single visit to a hive per month in which you deliberately subject yourself to these animals has a remarkably preserving effect as well as sapping the body of excessive urges: nature's own remedies are the best, don't you feel?

Yours, in physical and mental harmony
HRH The Prince of Wales

Jonathon Porritt
Friends of the Earth
26–28 Underwood Street
London
England   13 May 2006

Our time on Planet Earth may be short, Porritt, my old friend,
so I'll get straight to the point: I've been mulling over this for a
few days and just about reduced the thing to bullet points,
which I thought I'd run past your good self for suggestions. I
have a contention and it is this:

THE UK MONARCHY IS THE MOST ECO-EFFICIENT MEANS OF PRESIDING OVER THE COUNTRY

- Think about it: for one thing, we're unelected. This makes
  for huge paper savings in that it precludes the need for ballots
  every few years. Factor in the savings in timber – there's no
  need for ballot boxes, as well as lead savings – those little
  pencils, you know.

- Golden carriages are the most efficacious and environmentally
  'clean' way of getting about London.

- The Monarch only addresses the people once a year and then
  for ten minutes. There's none of this 24-hour Parliamentary
  Channel nonsense – an enormous saving in electricity.

Actually, that was all I could think of. Do you have any
more? Not to resort to 'sound bites', but I simply wish to point
out that those who would do away with us might well be
throwing away the baby of ecological sustainability with the
bathwater of impetuous Republicanism. Do you not agree? I
expect you must.

Yours, logically and ecologically
HRH The Prince of Wales

John Prescott
House of Commons
London
England   1 May 2008

I was a little put out to read that you have in the past suffered
from the eating disorder known as bulimia. As you probably
know my late, former wife was stricken by this disease and so I
have a little insight into what it involves. I just wished to say
this: if you should ever feel the need to talk, privately and
discreetly about your condition, then please do not hesitate to
seek out one of the many experienced counsellors qualified in
this field. I believe some of them may be in the phonebook.

>   Yours, concernedly
>   HRH The Prince of Wales

Peter Mandelson
House of Lords
London
England   6 June 2009

Congratulations, my Lord, on your elevation to the peerage.
I didn't think you socialists believed in taking ermine so it's
good to see one or two of you are prepared to take the 'broad
view'. I've followed your career with great interest from the
days when you sported that rather intriguing moustache to
your present eminence. That being so, I know you will take
what I'm about to say in the friendly and constructive way
it's intended.

I do fear you come across as a somewhat angular, malign
sort of fellow. When watching you on the television set, I can't

help but think of Cardinal Richelieu in his flowing red robes or
of some high-up cleric travelling across twelfth-century Europe
in a caravan, torturing deviants from the true faith. What can
be done to soften this a little, I wonder? I too have faced
'public image' difficulties. Have you, perhaps, considered
writing a children's book or visiting a discotheque and being
seen to 'let your hair down' within reasonable bounds, or taking
a very young wife? These are just thoughts.

>Yours, in elevation
>HRH The Prince of Wales

Nigel Farage
UK Independence Party
PO Box 408
Newton Abbot
Devon
England   17 November 2009

Dear Mr Farage

I want to make it clear from the 'outset' that I'm not a
political person. Some may think a greater integration with
Europe is a good thing; others, like yourself, disagree.
However, I was rather tickled by the following thought and
decided there was no harm in sharing it with you. You may
wish to use it on *Question Time*, a programme on which you
seem to appear on a fortnightly basis. You might deliver it
as follows:

>'I believe we're getting to the stage where Brussels
>bureaucrats will insist His Royal Highness Prince Charles,

the Prince of Wales, change the name of his estate "Poundbury" to "Eurobury".'

[Laughter]

When making this quip, I'd advise you to stick to it as written — otherwise, the rhythm of the comedy is put out.

I must reiterate that I do not have any declared position on Europe and would ask you do not accredit me with this joke. You might wish to make a donation of £25 to The Prince's Trust, however.

> Yours, in jest
> HRH The Prince of Wales

David Cameron
The Conservative Party
Millbank Tower
30 Millbank
London
England   8 May 2010

Dear Mr Cameron

I realise you Honourable Gentlemen are apt to cut up somewhat rusty at Royal interventions in political affairs, but in this delicate period of 'Hung Parliament' may I pitch in with a constructive suggestion — Con/Lib/Lab coalition?

Hang it all, it seems politics nowadays is a matter of slinging mud where we should be tilling the soil. It seems all three parties are agreed on the absolute basics — the need to go forward together, to do something about litter in the streets, getting young people out and about rather than frowsting indoors and rediscovering our spirituality as a kingdom.

Of course such a coalition would require a neutral leader so as not to get anyone's backs up. Such a person would need to be an outsider, not considered 'political' but someone who his entire adult life has been in contact with politicians of all hues, a man with some sort of vision (of Britain, in particular) and who is currently in search of some sort of role. Do any names spring to mind?

> Yours, and at your immediate disposal
> HRH The Prince of Wales

PS I know a fellow called 'Cameron' – one of the beaters at Balmoral. I expect you know him though curiously, he'd never heard of you.

Andrew Lansley
Secretary of State for Health
House of Commons
London
England   1 June 2010

Dear Mr Lansley

A number of my staff are wont to take 'cigarette breaks' throughout the day. I must say, one or two of them smoke desperately hard – I sometimes stare from my bay window on to the back courtyard and see them mumbling to each other and shaking their heads, no doubt in sadness at the state of the world. I've noticed, however, rummaging through my recycling bin that their packets are emblazoned with bold 'Health Warnings'.

I wonder if such warnings could not be attached to the sides of some of our modern buildings? Of course one would rather such carbuncles were banned but failing this, large inscriptions in black lettering reading, let's say, 'WARNING: THIS BUILDING EMPHASISES THE MECHANICAL OVER THE SPIRITUAL' or 'WARNING: THIS BUILDING MAY CAUSE A CERTAIN IMPOVERISHMENT OF THE INNER SELF' would do the job, I fancy. Could you have your team draw up some drafts? No hurry, anytime in the next fortnight would do.

Yours, in earnest
HRH The Prince of Wales

Nick Clegg
House of Commons
London
England   12 June 2010

Dear Mr Clegg

So, the Deputy Prime Minister of the United Kingdom, eh? Bet you didn't anticipate that one when the results came through on election night and 'Cleggmania' seemed as distant a memory as 'Osmond-mania'. But here you are, and there it is. We all hope you do a good job and stick to your principles, mobile as they are in this day and age of 'compromise'.

You know, Mr Clegg, you remind me of a boy with whom I was acquainted at Gordonstoun. His name, oddly enough, was 'Nick' or 'Nicky'. There we both were on the first day during breaktime. The other boys were laughing and playing various games – British Bulldog, Tag, Chinese Burns, that sort of thing . . . But we found it hard to join in and stood on our own, not able to make a connection with any of the other boys as they played; afraid, perhaps, that they'd tell us to go away and play somewhere else. One experiences loneliness in different ways and at different times in life but that sort of loneliness is the keenest sort, I always feel — young, estranged from parents and from one's supposed peers with nobody giving a damn.

I looked across at Nick. He was from another house, but he was in the same boat. We exchanged glances, half-smiled and shyly advancing towards each other along the chicken wire perimeter, mumbled our hellos and got talking. I felt a kinship with Nick: we had lots in common. We talked about Airfix, about hating being away from home and our favourite radio shows; we played word games like 'The Minister's Cat'. His company was a great comfort, a diversion. We spoke again over the next few days — we had a sort of tacit agreement: same time, same place. We agreed we'd look out for each other.

Then, on the fourth day I approached the spot and waited. Minutes passed, but no Nick. It was the same on the fifth. Perhaps he was sick, I thought. But then during the lunch break I was aware of two boys going around the playground, arms outstretched, chanting, 'All In For Kill The Prince!' Gradually, more and more boys joined them, forming a vanguard, their arms about each other's necks. And then they saw me by the fence and advanced on me like a cavalry charge. Among the faces bearing down on me were some familiar ones twisted with hateful relish: Tubby Braithwaite, 'Chips' Dennyson.

I looked around for Nick in the hope that he might appear from nowhere and spring to my defence. After all, we said we'd look out for each other. And suddenly, there he was. There he was, all right — he was one of the boys advancing on me. No flicker of recognition of me or my plight: his eyes were dead as he joined in the fury of the mob as they set on me, grabbing my ears, scraping their knuckles down the side of my head and pulling at my hair. 'Kill him, kill him!' they chanted — Nick loudest of all. I suppose he must have made some new friends. I suppose he must have decided it was better to be one of the boys who 'fitted in' and this was his way of showing it.

You betrayed me, Nick: I put my faith in you and you betrayed me. (Not you, Mr Clegg! Lost in the mists of the past there for a second . . .)

HRH The Prince of Wales

Boris Johnson
The London Assembly
London
England   1 October 2010

Dear Mr Johnson

Whenever I see you in the newspapers or on television, you're always 'out and about' on your bicycle. Well done! You're sending out a very positive, very green message to the people of London.

There's just one thing, however, and it's rather a delicate point: you are, it must be admitted, a person of rather generous proportions. I do fear people will look at you in your unfortunate physical condition and think to themselves, 'Well, cycling hasn't done him much good, has it? We might as well climb back in our Mondeos or Rovers.'

Would you consider going on a crash diet or high-intensity exercise programme that would get you into the sort of shape that helps ram home the message that cycling really does keep you trim?

Yours, in hope and expectation
HRH The Prince of Wales

Baroness Warsi
House of Lords
London
England   30 November 2010

Dear Baroness Warsi

I am writing to you in your capacity as a prominent British
Muslim. I know that you, like me, share the concern that
Muslims are not adequately represented in all walks of life in
Great Britain. You are prominent, you are British, you are
Muslim . . . As a bonus, you are even a woman. But we both
know, your presence could be greater. As an essentially peaceful
people, I believe Muslims have a great deal to offer British
society.

It concerns me greatly that there are, so far as I know, no
inner-city Muslim polo teams in the United Kingdom. I did
not encounter a single one all season and, given that the game
may well have originated in Asia (where it was known as *Chogan*)
it seems odd there has been so little take-up in such Muslim
strongholds as Dewsbury, Bradford, Luton and the Harehills
estate in Leeds.

If you were to provide horses and set up stables in these areas,
I would be happy to donate some old helmets, mallets and skid
boots I have which have seen better days, but would be adequate
for community regeneration purposes. Let's get the disaffected,
the underprivileged, on horseback and thirsting for the opening
chukka! And if there are no horses available, perhaps large dogs
could be used instead? Ideal for the smaller Muslim!

     Yours,
     HRH The Prince of Wales, Defender of Yourself (and
     Many Others)

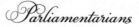

Theresa May
Home Secretary
House of Commons
London
England   10 December 2010

Dear Miss May

I must confess, both my wife and myself were thoroughly
shaken up by the events of last night. To have one's vehicle
manhandled and scraped by young men and women practically
red with rage, to hear cries for one's own decapitation, to be
temporarily uncertain of any escape route from the angry
throng . . . well, it sort of makes your life flash in front of
your eyes.

Most appalling was one of these malcontents managing to
set about my wife with a stick. A stick! That's what really 'sticks'
with me, if you'll pardon my pun. It's the irony of it, hang it
all. Like being attacked with a plant, or something. I've always
been pro the stick — ask my wife, ask Anne, anybody . . .
Whether whittled or in the form of a trusty staff, or propping
up a length of runner beans, I have always regarded the stick as
Man's Best Friend, not an assault weapon. Where did that idea
come from?

I'd be grateful, Miss May, if you could pass down
instructions that the next time these self-styled 'students' gather
with menace that the police impress upon them, using whatever
means of physical force they have at their disposal as necessary,
that a stick is not something you beat someone with.

Yours, with rigid resolve
HRH The Prince of Wales

Fellow Sportsmen (and Women)

Head of Sports
BBC TV
London
England   6 January 1972

Dear Sir

I cannot but help notice you honoured my sister Anne with the
'Sports Personality of the Year' award last month. I didn't
realise we 'Royals' were eligible, alongside the regular Tom,
Dick and Stirlings. Under these circumstances, one must
confess to feeling a little overlooked. I am a sportsman too, you
know. Polo's the game and if I say so myself, I'm rather good:
only yesterday, I scored with a pretty fine forehand in the third
chukka – straight from the knock-in. Might have scored more
but for a case of broken tack in the fourth chukka.

I also have a personality – I am rather a fan of *The Goons* and
like nothing more than getting 'out and about'. Could you
please bear me in mind for next year – why should Anne get all
the glory and not me? It hardly seems fair.

Keenly yours
HRH The Prince of Wales

Brian Clough
Derby County Football Club
Derby
England   17 June 1972

Dear Mr Clough

I write to you because we've a lot in common, you and me:
we've both been impersonated by Mr Mike Yarwood (with
varying degrees of success), we're dark-haired and we were born
before 1960. Actually, I'm struggling a little here but you see
my point. In winning the Association Football League with
Derby County Football Club, you've shown you're a man who
likes to get things done.

   Now, I'm not writing to you for 'soccer tips' – I'm afraid
when it comes to your game, I've long since shown myself to
have 'two left feet'. What I was looking for was vocal skills. I'm
impressed by the way your voice carries – every word seems to
hover in the air for a second or so after it's left your mouth. I
don't suppose you've noticed but when I talk, my words seem to
tighten – they emerge as if wearing stiff collars and tight shoes.
So, instead of 'outward bound', I'll say 'iteward bind'. I've tried
to eradicate the thing in front of the mirror – Prince Andrew
caught me the other day, chanting, 'ITE! ITE! ITE! ITE!
ITE!' – and guffawed in that carrying way of his. Trying to say
'OUT!', you see, but to no avail.

   So, what do you say, 'Big Lad?' I'm proposing a course in
vocal tuition. After three months, I want to surprise my polo
team-mates by declaring in your own, stentorian manner,
'FOR MISSING FROM THERE, YOU WANT BLOODY
SHOOTING!' Primarily it's the emphasis I like, as opposed to
that Northern coarseness, amusing as it is in its proper place.

           Yours, vocally
           HRH The Prince of Wales

Jonny Wilkinson
c/o Rugby Football Union
Rugby House
Twickenham Stadium
Twickenham
Middlesex
England   20 December 2003

Dear Mr Wilkinson

'Jonny Wilkinson drops for World Cup Glory! . . . ' Yes, I
listened to the commentary on my transistor radio and, along
with the rest of the United Kingdom, threw my cap in the air as
I imagined the rugger pill sailing over the bar for three vital
points against our Commonwealth friends and sporting rivals,
the Australians.

In your case, Rugby Union was clearly character building. If
that is the case, then in the light of my rugger playing days at
Gordonstoun, I should be the greatest character on earth. For
me, the scrum wasn't an exciting goal-scoring opportunity but a
sort of makeshift torture chamber, in which one was subject to
every conceivable poke, hack, discreet but eye-wateringly
painful toe-punt, rabbit punch and tweak. Whenever the ball
came to me, I was at once trampled over as if by an army
retreating at speed in hobnail boots across a tin bridge.

I do not know what it is to watch a ball sail over the bar for a
conversion but I do know how the ball felt; on one occasion, in
an inter-form challenge, I was physically hurled over the bar
itself by an older, burlier boy – Reggie Bagshaw – like some
tossed human caber. The referee turned a blind eye and when I
told my father about the incident, he got up from the table and
strode down the corridor, his belly laugh echoing long and loud
behind him. In short, Wilkinson, even as I whooped, I winced.
I trust you understand.

Yours, in both pleasure and pain
HRH The Prince of Wales

Fellow Sportsmen (and Women)

Jonny Wilkinson
c/o Rugby Football Union
Rugby House
Twickenham Stadium
Twickenham
Middlesex
England   29 December 2003

Dear Mr Wilkinson

Further to my letter of the other day, which I trust you received
safely, one other point: as I mentioned, I'm a 'rugger man'
myself and my father, Prince Philip, would now and again come
and shout exhortations to me from the touchline. I can't in all
honesty say I always relished this.

'Take the bull by the balls, boy!' he used to cry out. 'You've
must take the bull by the balls!' Taken literally, that always
struck me as an ill-advised thing to do – you might well anger
the beast. Got to admit, it left me confused rather than
encouraged, and inside a scrum with form boys ill-disposed
towards you at the best of times is not a place to be beset by
confusion.

What do you think he was driving at? Is it some more widely
used rugger term? Did you ever get it? If so, I hope it proved
more of a 'spur' to you than me.

Yours, &c
HRH The Prince of Wales

José Mourinho
Chelsea FC
Stamford Bridge
London
England   8 September 2004

Dear Mr Mourinho

Hola! I notice I've yet to welcome you to the United Kingdom –
very remiss of me, but 'better late than never'. I can't help
noticing, however, that you have become notorious for
declaring yourself to be 'the special one' and carrying yourself
with a certain, haughty arrogance.

I'd advise against this. You will find us an essentially modest
people, not given to 'swanking' and you will not achieve any
kind of success in England if you carry on in this way. It is not
our custom. In fact, your football club might even run the risk
of 'relegation'. I'd commend you to study the example of our
English managers – Graham Taylor, for example. Watch how he
carries himself, and learn.

Instructively, yours
HRH The Prince of Wales

Fellow Sportsmen (and Women)

Miss Paula Radcliffe, MBE
c/o The Amateur Athletics Association
London
England   20 April 2005

Dear Miss Radcliffe

I was sorry to hear of the toilet mishap during your latest race.
I happened to have left the room when it occurred, but Prince
Harry described the incident to me in excessive detail on my
return and I sympathise. Once, during the second chukka of a
vital Polo game on which the season hinged, I found myself
quite unaccountably and urgently seized by a Call of Nature.
And it was, I fear, Mr Brown and several members of his family
who were knocking at the door.

It seemed impossible, that I would be overwhelmed at any
second, but I thought of Rorke's Drift and the English spirit
that maintains the garrison in the face of intense pressure. I
stiffened every sinew and held out for the vital three minutes
whereupon I dismounted. Knees almost buckling, I somehow
made my way to a 'Portaloo', where I experienced perhaps the
most profound sensation of relief I have ever known in my time
on this earth. Indeed, I wonder if, sitting in that rather smelly,
cramped and barely sanitary cubicle, I came as close as I ever
have to true happiness in this life. (I suppose I shall be dubbed
a hypocrite as an advocate of ecological causes for not taking a
spade, digging a hole and voiding into it, but believe me, there
simply wasn't the 'time'.)

Next time this happens, think of my example. Then, like
me, you will avoid making an utter fool of yourself in public.

Yours, in sympathy
HRH The Prince of Wales

David Beckham
c/o The English Football Association
Soho Square
London
England   23 June 2008

Dear Mr Beckham

First of all, allow me to thank you once again for participating
in my Highgrove Impromptu Five-A-Side-A-Thon which,
you'll be gratified to know, raised £2,000 for the local
underprivileged – which I hope will be spent wisely on their
behalf. I apologise again for the roughness of some of the
young Prince Harry's tackles, particularly the one necessitating
your hobbling off for a touch of the 'Magic Sponge'. The boy is
red-haired and impetuous (I'm not sure where he gets it from).
I trust the crocus-derived balm I advised you to rub into the
affected area did the trick?

I write because I happened to be in New York recently and
was most taken aback to see a rather gigantic poster of you
draped across the frontage of the department store Macy's,
clad in nothing but a pair of somewhat snug undergarments. I
trust you won't be disconcerted when I tell you I had my driver
linger at the spot as I looked you up and down in fascination
until the build-up of Manhattan traffic expressed itself in
a raucous ejaculation of horns and we pootled on up
34th Street.

Later, in my hotel suite, I stared at myself clad only in briefs
in a full-length mirror and realised how short I fall of the
physical ideal. Hang it all, I'm a middle-aged man but there must
be something I can do to get closer to being the model 'muscular
Christian' (or muscular Defender of Many Faiths)? I was
wondering, therefore – could you perhaps look in again next
time you're in the country and perhaps devise a routine that

really puts me through my physical paces? In return, I could give you some tips about public speaking. I'm afraid you do have a habit of lapsing into some sort of Estuary mumble — I could help you with this.

Yours, hopefully
HRH The Prince of Wales

David Beckham
c/o The English Football Association
Soho Square
London
England   25 June 2008

Dear Mr Beckham

Last night, I had the strangest dream. In it, I had taken the place of yourself on that giant billboard in New York, resplendent and strapping in my underwear — and it was me who received a letter from you asking if I would help you get up to physical scratch for your next football game. I was thoroughly disconcerted by the request — it made me understand how you might have felt on receiving the same request from me in real life. On that basis, perhaps we had best forget this correspondence ever took place, don't you feel?

Yours, &c
HRH The Prince of Wales

Sir Alex Ferguson
Manchester United Football Club
Old Trafford
Manchester
England   7 September 2010

Dear Sir Alex

Hoots! It's a braw wee problem ye've got with the big feller Mr
Rooney, I say. (It's OK, I'm a Balmoral resident, I can banter
on like this without causing offence — none of my ghillies do.)
Man to man, however, I'd advise indulgence. He's a young man
and as my Uncle Louis used to say, young men need to sow
their wild oats. I know I sowed my oats! It'll be the same for this
Wayne. Of course, that was before I was married . . . But once I
was married, I settled down, er, well, for a while. Anyway, oats,
I think, is what it's all about. As a Scotchman I daresay you've
had a few oats in your time so you'll understand. I trust this has
been helpful. I'd write on, but I'm a busy man and I expect you
are too.

Yours, in Caledonian camaraderie
HRH The Prince of Wales

   PS Your face seems to have cleared up dramatically. Is
there a cream you might recommend? The bark I was
advocated as a scrub only seems to be making mine worse,
despite being organic. Actually, ignore all that stuff about
oats — just small talk, really, working up to the thing about
the cream. Between you and me, I don't give a hang about
Association Football.

Fellow Sportsmen (and Women)

Richard Keys and Andy Gray
c/o Sky Sports
London
England   20 January 2011

Dear Mr Keys and Mr Gray

I'm sending this to 'Sky' on the assumption that despite your 'contretemps', they'll at least still forward your mail.

You'll forgive me, I trust, but I must admit that until a few days ago, I hadn't the faintest idea who the pair of you were but now you're both on the scrapheap, I very much do. Funny thing, life, don't you feel? Anyway, having witnessed the events of the last few days, with certain remarks you've been caught making off-camera concerning young women 'smashing it' and 'do me a favour', I thought a few avuncular words from a wise old hand might be welcome.

I've seen a lot of talk about the dangers of this sort of thing and of falling victim to a new 'Thought Police' in this 'politically correct' world we live in. Believe me, I understand. I have thoughts – I often have thoughts. Many of us do, I believe . . . long, hard thoughts. But notice how I do not tell you what these thoughts are and so, thoughts they remain. There, I believe, you came a cropper for it was not the 'Thought Police' you fell foul of, but the 'Actually Came Out And Said Police'. A different branch, so to speak, of the Force.

I do hope this is of some comfort to you as you seek fresh employment – I visited a Labour Exchange once, you know. Fascinating!

Constructively, yours
HRH The Prince of Wales

Andy Murray
c/o The All England Lawn Tennis and Croquet Club
Wimbledon
London
England   4 June 2011

So, once again, you've 'come' a cropper at Wimbledon. You must feel some days that it is simply never going to happen for you. It's certainly beginning to look that way, isn't it? I know that feeling — in fact, I have been rather gloomily prey to it just lately.

In the spirit, then of making lemonade of the lemons life hands one, I have a proposition. It seems that, like yourself, our young people are going to have to get used to the idea that they are simply not going to be able to realise the dreams they might have, their own 'Wimbledons', so to speak. In their case, I'm thinking of, you know, going to university, buying their own house, that sort of thing.

Can I suggest that, working together, we devise a series of seminars under the banner of REDUCING EXPECTATIONS – PREPARING FOR DISAPPOINTMENT. We would be the keynote speakers, advising the young on how to cope with the inevitability that for them, life is likely to be a series of crushing setbacks and the sooner they get used to the idea, the better. With your rather surly, morose manner, you would, I think, be perfectly suited to 'convey' this message. I hope that compliment does not make you blush!

    Defeatedly, yours
    HRH The Prince Of Wales

Deep Thinkers, Eminences of the Higher Arts

Sir John Betjeman
Poet Laureate   1 June 1976

Dear Sir John

As you recall, I wrote to you in May in my capacity as chairman of the King George Jubilee Trust to compose upon the occasion of my mother, Her Majesty The Queen's Jubilee Year. I was hoping you could dash off one of your perfectly formed bits of scansion in honour of the twenty-fifth anniversary of HM accession to the Throne.

Yesterday, I saw your effort and I must confess, I was somewhat dismayed. As Father might say, it was as if you really hadn't put your back into it. You are Laureate, and with that comes honour and a stipend. In return we do expect a bit more effort. As an Englishman, you must rejoice in my mother's long reign – you are jubilant, surely? One would not guess as much from lines like, '25 years/Gosh, is that how long it's been?/Since you first became Queen/From Salisbury to Slough/We do salute thou'. I don't want to be picky, but shouldn't it be 'thee' and not 'thou' – which I suspect you only brought in so as to rhyme with 'Slough'. And what is it, Sir, with you and Slough?

May I ask you to have another run-up at it – I'd hate to have to rope in Pam Ayres as 'substitute'.

> Yours, in mild disappointment tempered with hope
> HRH The Prince of Wales

Jean-Paul Sartre
c/o The Louvre
Paris
France   20 April 1978

Dear Mr Sartre

I'm afraid I don't have your address, but I daresay you look in
now and again at the Louvre and someone there will spot you
and pass this on to you.

I'm very interested in your philosophy of 'Existentialism'.
I've tried to 'bone up' on it, but there were certain excessively
wordy passages I had to skip over. It seems to me that the nub of
what you're saying is all to do with the art, or idea of 'being' –
hence the title of your book, *Being And Nothingness*.

Now it strikes me that the weakness of your ideas comes
down to this whole concept of 'being' – being, as it were, the
be-all and end-all of things. But here is the difference between
my philosophy and yours (and where I like to think I have the
upper hand): yours is all about 'being', mine is about 'doing'.
Anyone can sit about and simply 'be' all day. Some indeed
would not so much call it 'being' as shirking! But 'doing' –
getting things done? That's a much tougher proposition. It's
what I look to do.

You must understand, M Sartre, that you argue things from
an 'intellectual' position whereas under the influence of
Laurens van der Post, I argue from the non-intellectual realm
of the mind. Mind you, 'hell is other people' – I must agree
about that. Bloody journalists, especially – so at least you have
something right!

Yours, in *liberté* et *fraternité*
HRH The Prince of Wales

The Prince Charles Letters

Laurens van der Post
c/o The British Library
London
England   13 September 1980

Sir

You remain my guiding light, my inspiration in a world
rendered foggy by the exhaust fumes of the toxic modern age.
You once wrote the following: 'We behave as if there were some
magic in mere thought, and we use thinking for purposes for
which it was never designed. As a result we are no longer
sufficiently aware of what we cannot know intellectually, what we
must know in other ways, of the living experience before and
beyond our transitory knowledge'. I must say, I'd never thought
of that before (is it a good or a bad thing, would you say?) but it
certainly made a terrific impression on me.

And so yesterday, I decided to give it a try. Not thinking,
that is: to sit down and empty one's mind of all thoughts, switch
off the mental engine; experience just living for a change. It's
jolly difficult – like squashing moles with a mallet! No sooner
has one put one down and another pops out of another hole.
I'd nearly 'cracked it' when out of nowhere, the 'Ying Tong
Song' by The Goons – do you know it? – tootled through my
head like a bally earworm and tiddle-eye-po, I was 'back at
square one'.

Any tips? Maybe I wasn't sitting properly. Should I squat,
perhaps? Trouble is, squatting hurts my lower back after a while.

Your faithful disciple
HRH The Prince of Wales

Ted Hughes
Poet Laureate
Devon
England   16 June 1987

Dear Mr Hughes

It has been said you write of 'The struggle in the soil as well as
the soul'. This has been well said of your verse and as a 'soil and
soul' man myself, I fully concur. However, there is another
struggle which I confess I have undergone in perusing your
latest work: lines commissioned to commemorate my brother
Edward's *It's A Royal Knockout*, which historians may well count as a
crucial moment in the relationship between Monarch and the
Common Man. It's the struggle to work out what in blazes
you're on about!

I've read the whole thing and while there's a great deal about
owls and otters, the recurring misadventures of a crow
entangled in a mesh of brambles, not to mention a ferret
mauling a pregnant rabbit, I could find no direct reference to
the television revelries – which, after all, were at the heart of
the brief in the first place.

And hang it all, I know you're modern and so forth, but
would a rhyme or two here and there really hurt so much? I
suspect this aversion to rhyme, like modern music's aversion to
tunes, is some sort of slacking, an avoidance of the real hard
work of composition. Could you please take another look at it –
once more, with rhymes? (I'd help you out, but the only thing I
can think of that rhymes with 'Edward' is 'dead wood' and of
course that isn't at all suitable.)

Yours, &c
HRH The Prince of Wales

Alan Bennett
c/o The National Theatre
London
England   12 August 1994

Dear Mr Bennett

I was rather taken by your film *The Madness Of King George* —
certainly plenty of food for one's noggin there, especially for a
future monarch. Is one on or off one's rocker? How would one
know? Would one's staff bring to it to one's attention if one
showed marked and perturbing signs of eccentricity? It is
gratifying to note thus far none of them has.

    In that confidence, and also to counterbalance the King
George thing, I was wondering — would you consider it worth
your while to compose a companion play entitled *The Sensibleness
of Prince Charles*? It would cover my thoughts on balancing the
need to modernise with the horrors of modernity, of enjoying
harmony with nature even as one is massacring its specimens
and so forth. I am of course assuming you think my ideas
sensible — happily, men and women generally seem to take this
view. Don't mention that I gave you the idea, should this come
to fruition — it might seem immodest.

        Discreetly yours
        HRH The Prince of Wales

Tracey Emin
c/o Tate Modern
Bankside
London SE1   6 January 2000

Dear Miss Emin

You've been drawn to my attention as a 'Young British Artist'.
I'm rather an old British artist myself, but as such hope that I
can pass on the benefit of my experience.

I've seen you on the television set more than once and both
times you appeared 'sozzled'. To me, this is symptomatic of the
whole modern art movement, one that is dissipated, has rather
lost its way and weaves unsteadily and uncertainly rather than
moving forward. (Of course it is a maxim of mine that in order
to move forward, you have to move backwards.) Everything
about your work — I'm thinking of this 'unmade bed' exhibit, in
particular — smacks of slacking and a lack of fresh air. I suggest
that tomorrow morning, when you get out of your bed, don't
think of the resulting mess of duvet and crumpled sheets as 'a
work of art' but work that needs to be done. Make that bed
(remember, pillows plumped and 'hospital corners') and then
armed with easel and watercolours, take the next coach out into
the countryside, find the nearest waterfall and let your brush
yomp freely, but figuratively across the canvas.

You'll soon realise this whole 'Modern Art' thing is an
adolescent fad, something you 'get out of your system' — like
Donny Osmond or 'Little Jimmy' Osmond, or even dressing
up as a Nazi. Things look the way they are because that's how
they're supposed to look — that's what Picasso failed to
understand.

　　　　Yours, in perspective
　　　　HRH The Prince of Wales

Vidal Sassoon
60 South Molton Street
London
England   12 May 2002

Dear Mr Sassoon

I'm writing to you as Britain's leading hair man but I'm not
asking for a makeover, far from it! It's just that, with respect,
you and oneself – well, we're on opposing sides of the
spectrum. You see, you believe in fashion. And yes, fashion has
been kind to you: it has made you your 'boodle'. However, I do
not believe in fashion because you see, Mr Sassoon, fashions
change. They are here today, gone tomorrow. Has that ever
occurred to you?

      Now, take my own hairstyle. It has never been fashionable.
One unkind writer once remarked that it looked as if it had
been splurged on to my head using a Mr Whippy ice-cream
dispenser. I can laugh off such remarks because my hair
represents continuity. I have maintained it since I was twelve
years old: it has outlasted several prime ministers, seen off
rock'n'roll, The Beatles, the teddy boys, the punk rockers and
everything else they've tried to throw at it.

      What I was proposing was a public platform, a friendly if
frank and open debate between us to touch on the issues raised
in this letter. When would you be available for such an event?
I'd appreciate a quick response because by this time next week, I
may well have forgotten I ever wrote this letter at all – this
sometimes happens, as things stack up – and it would be a pity
to miss this opportunity. Hair today, gone tomorrow, you
might say!

            Unfashionably, yours
            HRH The Prince of Wales

Stephen Fry
c/o The British Broadcasting Corporation
London
England   23 August 2003

Dear Stephen

Just a note to thank you for your excellent company last
Wednesday evening — I wish I could have written down half of
the clever things you said as we dined. Next time I must bring a
pen and paper, or perhaps have one of my staff sit in discreetly
and take notes.

One thing has rather stuck with me, however — this idea of
yours that the word 'moist' is one of the funniest words in the
English language. I must confess I don't quite see it. I've said it
over and over to myself in the hope of raising a chuckle but with
no luck. I was even repeating it to myself in front of the
bathroom mirror last night: 'Moist', 'Moist', 'Moist' . . . No
joy. One of my staff caught me at it as he came in to rinse my
toothbrush — he must have left with the impression that I'm a
bit of an eccentric. Perhaps this is one occasion where your
acclaimed sense of humour has deserted you? How about
'knobbly knees'? Hardy perennials in the garden of comedy,
those two words, I've always thought!

Yours, in fun
HRH The Prince of Wales

Norman Foster
Foster + Partners
London
England   12 July 2004

OK, Foster,

No formalities, no small talk, straight down to cases! We've not always seen eye-to-eye regarding the horrors of modern architecture but hitherto I felt there was a seabed of civility in our exchanges, a certain mutual respect. You'll know that a few years ago I wrote to you suggesting if significant tracts of land within the centre of London were turned into allotments, specifically vegetable patches, this would release the choke-hold of modern life and its tyranny of steel, concrete and glass and afford us a much-needed reminder of the fruits of the soil amid the hurly-burly of commerce.

I did not receive a reply from you, which I considered rum. And then just this week, while being driven along Leadenhall Street, I glanced up at St Mary's Axe only to be confronted with what I can only describe as a giant gherkin staring down at me.

I see now there was never any seabed of civility between us and I see what has happened: you noted my stress on vegetables and this is your snide retort! It's not architecture — this is a vertical act of sarcasm at my expense. Well, it has not gone unnoticed. I shall be keeping a keen eye on the architectural landscape and I warn you, if I spot any similarly vegetable-shaped erections — a turnip-shaped HQ for a Japanese Bank, or a mushroom-resembling conference centre — then I shall not spare you the caustic end of my tongue, either in correspondence or on the television set.

> Yours, more in sorrow than anger (well,
> actually quite angry)
> HRH The Prince of Wales

Stephen Fry
c/o BBC Television Centre
London
England   24 August 2004

Dear Stephen

I'm sending this to the BBC as I assume you have your own
pigeonhole there. I wanted to 'touch base' with you as I rather
hoped to get you down to Highgrove at your earliest
convenience to help me look over some ideas I've had for a
'Plants Chatroom' on the Web. If you were to lend the
considerable weight of your celebrity to endorse the project,
I'm sure it would be of mutual benefit, enhancing your own
prestige into the bargain.

      Yours, &c
      HRH The Prince of Wales

Stephen Fry
c/o BBC Television Centre
London
England   25 August 2004

Dear Stephen

I have still to hear back from you regarding the 'Plants
Chatroom' project. One of my staff contacted your agency and
they said you were currently flat-out on a new series of *QI*, three
voiceovers (including a commercial for windscreen wiper
fluid), a children's cartoon series about a feisty guinea pig, two
video games, a documentary on penguins and parts in five

feature films currently 'in development'; also a twelve-part
radio series looking back on the history of the word 'Arse'.

You *are* a busy man! I thought you made your pile writing a
musical. Is all this work altogether healthy? Balanced? Surely
your soul cries out for the respite of Highgrove? I have two
slide shows you have yet to see.

Yours, &c
HRH The Prince of Wales

Stephen Fry
c/o BBC Television Centre
London
England   2 February 2005

Dear Stephen

More than five months now and still no word back on my
'Plants Chatroom' idea. According to your agency, you are
working on a new series of *QI*, a pilot for a situation comedy for
American television based on *The Importance of Being Earnest*, a
sixteen-part travel documentary in which you criss-cross South
America by taxi, recording a jazz-funk fusion album with your
friends Hugh Laurie and Jo Brand, plus rehearsals for a
pantomime season in Kettering. Oh, and a book entitled *A
Complete and Utter History of Every Last Lovely Little Bit of the World*, in
which you document absolutely everything ever done by
anybody in your own inimitable style. A thought briefly crossed
my mind that you only take on so much work to avoid coming
down to Highgrove, but I fear one is becoming far too "cynical"
in one's old age – you're not, are you?

Yours, &c
HRH The Prince of Wales

Richard Dawkins
c/o New College
Oxford
England   19 February 2008

Dear Mr Dawkins

On Stephen Fry's recommendation, I've been reading one or
two of your books. I trust you'll permit me the liberty of doing
what we Royals generally aren't supposed to do and that's
'answer back'– as the Defender of many faiths, white, black,
brown, yellow, green. And here is my devastating rejoinder to
your entire book. I trust you are sitting down because what I
have to say may come as a shock. It is this:

> In arguing your case so fervently, you yourself are as
> fundamentalist as the very fundamentalists you attack.

I'm sorry if that's 'wrecked' your argument. Perhaps you'd
care to join us for one of our inter-faith tea and samosas
evenings at Highgrove to discuss your theories with the Imams?
You'll find them essentially peaceful people. They have ancient
wisdom on their side, so don't be surprised if you come
unstuck – and hang it all, when you do, don't start jumping up
and down! You may believe we are descended from monkeys
but that's no reason to act like one (you have a reputation for
getting extremely truculent, you know). I can sense you getting
hot under the collar as you read this, right now. Well, don't!
For Heaven's sake man, calm down and pull yourself together.

Yours, &c
HRH The Prince of Wales

Business, Technology and Other Necessary Carbuncles

Attn Tim Berners-Lee
Internet HQ
London
England   6 February 1999

Dear Mr Berners-Lee

I'm informed you are the person who invented the 'Internet'
and are therefore, as it were, in overall charge of the operation.

Quite honestly, I'm unaccustomed to what's involved in
handling this sort of technology. In particular, I find the
directions on the 'Internet' rather brusque. 'Enter', 'Search', 'Log
In' – it's like being addressed by a surly robot. Would it be a stretch
to ask if you could devise a programme for my own personal use in
which commands read: 'Enter, Your Highness', or 'Log In, Your
Highness'? If that's too much, a simple 'Sir' would do. Am I being
stuffy? I asked my staff and they really didn't think so.

> Your humble servant
> HRH The Prince of Wales

Steve and Julie Pankhurst
Friends Reunited
Barnet
Hertfordshire
England   13 September 2002

Dear Mr and Mrs Pankhurst

I do hope you won't consider this too awful a stretch, but it's a
matter of some delicacy and concerns this 'Friends Reunited'
website. You see, I was rather thinking of, well, looking in.

What did happen to some of the fellows at Gordonstoun — 'Tubby' Mosthorpe, for instance? He and a chum of his once nailed me, in full uniform, to the inside of one of the lavatory doors during my ablutions. Or 'Todger' Ffiennes? He once punctured my hot water bottle with a tin-tac so that it leaked ever so slowly during the night. I remember waking, damp and crimson with shame, convinced I'd had a personal accident and cutting down to the boiler room to burn my pyjamas in the furnace rather than shove them in the laundry basket and risk cross-examination from Matron. Unfortunately, the janitor caught me in there and I had to explain my actions, which in fairness must have come across as a bit bizarre, in front of the entire school at assembly.

Anyway, I'd like to find out what happened to these friends. Perhaps they went on to great things — perhaps they didn't. Perhaps they got embroiled in scandals or nasty accidents — I should like to know. Perhaps they died, brutally and violently, deservedly even — who knows? I would be curious to find out.

The question is, do I have to 'log on' as HRH The Prince of Wales, or could I go about the site under the guise of a pseudonym, like Henry V the night before Agincourt? 'Charlie Leroy', perhaps? The African-Caribbean air of that name would probably put most people 'off the scent'.

> Discreetly, yours
> 'Charlie Leroy' (aka HRH The Prince of Wales)

The Prince Charles Letters

The Chief Executive
Colgate
Guildford Business Park
Middleton Road
Guildford
Surrey
England   2 May 2003

Dear Sir

I don't know where it came from — none of my staff, I'm sure,
whose loyalty is a byword — but it has somehow reached the
public domain that I do not place my own toothpaste on the
brush myself, but have my man do it for me. It's beneath my
dignity to comment on this frivolous matter and I shan't do so
here. More seriously, it does concern me greatly, as I'm sure it
does yourself (albeit for commercial reasons), that people of all
ages are simply not cleaning their teeth as often as they should.
As a country, we're lagging behind.

What I propose is that with your sponsorship, I take part
in a public information film demonstrating the virtues and
correct method of teeth cleaning. I think a short film of the
future King taking care of his dental hygiene at the washbasin,
perhaps in a pair of stripy pyjamas for verisimilitude, would
prove not uninteresting to people up and down the country. My
friend Mrs Parker Bowles certainly seems to think so. 'Oh,
they'd watch, all right!' she eventually declared, having
swallowed her muesli the wrong way when I put the idea to her.

Perhaps if you could come back with some mutually
convenient dates my man and I could drive down to your
studios for the afternoon and we could do the demonstration
to camera. I would provide my own pyjamas.

              Hygienically, yours
              HRH The Prince of Wales

Professor Colin Pillinger
Planetary Science Department
The Open University
Milton Keynes
England   18 February 2004

Dear Professor Pillinger

I must say, Professor Pillinger, that with your muttonchops and optimism, one cannot help but take a shine to you. I understand you had a pop at launching some sort of device to land on Mars but the thing went rather skew-wiff, ending up somewhere in the silly mid-off of the solar system rather than bang on the stumps. Still, we are English (and of course, Scottish, Irish and, last but not least, Welsh) and we persevere, moving forward together.

May I suggest, however, that you change the name of the dog after which our mission is named? Beagle 2? Beagles do not inspire as we gaze in wonderment at the Heavens. We need a hound that will elevate man's soul, not one that in the popular imagination lies all day on top of a kennel. But which dog? Irish Setter? No! Poodle? No! Corgi? Oh, no! How about Spaniel? That seems the best of the bunch so far. If I think of others, I shall drop you a further line. Alsatian?

>   Yours, looking to the Heavens
>   HRH The Prince of Wales

Professor Colin Pillinger
Planetary Science Department
The Open University
Milton Keynes
England   19 February 2004

Bull mastiff? Great Dane?

     Yours, &c
     HRH The Prince of Wales

Professor Colin Pillinger
Planetary Science Department
The Open University
Milton Keynes
England   20 February 2004

Basset hound?

     Yours, &c
     HRH The Prince of Wales

Professor Colin Pillinger
Planetary Science Department
The Open University
Milton Keynes
England   21 February 2004

Collie?

     Yours, &c
     HRH The Prince of Wales

Professor Colin Pillinger
Planetary Science Department
The Open University
Milton Keynes
England   22 February 2004

Staffordshire Terrier?

      Yours, &c
      HRH The Prince of Wales

Professor Colin Pillinger
Planetary Science Department
The Open University
Milton Keynes
England   23 February 2004

Coarse-haired hound?

      Yours, &c
      HRH The Prince of Wales

Professor Colin Pillinger
Planetary Science Department
The Open University
Milton Keynes
England   24 February 2004

Dear Professor Pillinger

I've made the most embarrassing discovery: due to a clerical
error at my end, I never actually sent a letter intended for you
on 18 February, which must make all the 'follow-up'
correspondence you've since received from me, essentially a list
of dogs, seem rather confusing. I enclose a copy of the original
letter.

> Regretfully, yours
> HRH The Prince of Wales

Mervyn King
The Bank of England
Threadneedle Street
London
England   12 June 2006

Dear Mr King

Well, it's sad to dwell on this fact but sooner or later, my
mother will no longer be with us and then we must be in place
to deal with the implications for banknotes and the coinage of
the realm. All notes and loose change bearing the image of Her
Majesty The Queen will have to be phased out as quickly as
possible and replaced by currency bearing my own

countenance. This will be quite an operation — I trust you and
your staff have contingency plans!

Might I suggest that in order to save time you send some of
your best people — your artists and etchers — down to Highgrove
so that we can discuss profiles and poses for use on future
currency. I think we should do this now while I'm still in
reasonably good physical 'nick'. For the banknotes, I have a
variety of suggestions:

£5: Charles at his easel, looking to a distant stag for inspiration
£10: Charles staring beyond the horizon, enraptured by his
own 'Vision of Britain'
£20: Charles with rifle at half-cock, having just shot the stag he
painted earlier

Of course, your people will doubtless have their own
suggestions but I think I prefer mine.

>Yours, in 'sterling' support
>HRH The Prince of Wales

Alan Sugar
The British Broadcasting Corporation
London
England   11 December 2008

Dear Mr Sugar

'You're fired!'

I trust you don't mind my little joke. You're not fired, of
course — far from it. In any case, I can't fire you until I've
actually hired you, though come to think of it, it confuses the

dickens out of me that you do the same to those young people on your television show: fire them before you've even hired them, that is to say.

Well, that opening line didn't work at all, but at least it's broken the 'ice'. I have a business idea I thought you might be interested in investing in: we've all heard of tin openers, but what about a tin closer? The idea is, having opened a tin of, say, ketchup, and finding you don't use all of it, with this clever little electrical device you can weld the lid back into its place in one simple, circular action, resealing it so that the ketchup can be used another day.

Perhaps you could put it to the rest of your colleagues in the 'Dragon's Den'?

> Hopefully, yours
> HRH The Prince of Wales

Richard Branson
Virgin Group, Ltd.
London
England   5 June 2009

Dear Mr Branson

I should like to thank you once again for your message in support of my campaign to Protect the Rainforests. It is absolutely vital, I think, that big businessmen like yourself lend your weight to such campaigns — it assists tremendously in putting across our message. And it also helps that you have a beard — it reassures the 'ordinary chap'. As does the fact that you do not go about the place wearing a top hat, monocle and long fur coat, which again means a great, great deal.

I hope that you will remain a supporter of such causes well into the future. For that to be so, it's vital you don't 'lag behind' commercially. I would urge you, therefore, to really pep up your energies in expanding Virgin products — the vodka, the mobile phones, the limousine services, the luxury vacations, the fizzy drinks, the prophylactics and of course, the airlines. Build more planes, more holiday destinations . . . be 'number one'. Only this way can you successfully keep up the high profile that lends credibility to campaigns such as mine, encouraging people to reduce their carbon footprint and consume less.

Consistently, yours
HRH The Prince of Wales

Tony Hayward
BP
1 St James's Square
London
England   29 May 2010

Dear Mr Hayward

You know, it's really a frightful mess that you fellows have created off the American seaboard, don't you think? I'd say! Mother Nature's ire has been provoked and once again, it makes one yearn for the days of loom, smock and spinney before all this combustion and lubrication, which makes modern life such a choking hell for many of us.

The incident reminds me of the time when I was five and playing 'hoop and stick' outside the study, where Mother was composing a letter to the Ambassador of what was then

Rhodesia. A footman was delivering ink on a tray to replenish
the Royal well and at a point of high involvement in the game, I
slipped on the carpet, sending footman, bottle and tray directly
into the clasp of poor Mater, resulting in a black mess similar
to the one you've made. Nothing was said but dripping with
ink, she gave me a look which registered profound dismay at my
misadventures, one that I feel has persisted to this day.

Still, now we must knuckle down to a solution and I
propose this: giant, waterproof ink blotters lowered with
mechanical devices on to the seabed. The practicalities I leave
to you – the hard bit, I often find, is thinking these things up.
Keep me updated as to progress, would you.

> Practically, yours
> HRH The Prince of Wales

Julian Assange
c/o The Embassy of Sweden
11 Montagu Place
London
England   1 December 2010

Dear Mr Assange

It's not for a personage like myself to express an opinion on the
rights and wrongs of leaking confidential documents, which
may or may not be in the public interest. However, I do make
one request of you, not as a Prince but as a private citizen and a
concerned son.

It may be that top-secret documents have fallen into your
hands regarding my father, HRH The Prince Philip. If they
have done so, they may well reveal a side of his character

unknown to citizens of the Kingdom. You see, it's like this. My father has rather a jaundiced attitude towards foreigners, particularly those of different skin hues. It's not that he's against foreigners exactly, just that he finds them inherently amusing in a way that, were they to get wind of it, they might well find insulting. At my 50th birthday party, for example, I overheard him making a general remark about members of the Indian subcontinent ('they get everywhere!'), which might be misinterpreted as comparing them with an infestation.

Needless to say, if this were to get out it'd be dynamite and cause no end of trouble, as well as profoundly alter the public perception of Father. I urge you, if you have any lingering feelings for the Empire, to 'sit on this one'. I'd be greatly obliged.

Yours, hopefully
HRH The Prince of Wales

Sir Philip Green
Topshop
Oxford Street
London
England   21 January 2011

Dear Sir Philip

Twenty-four hours later but still no response from you regarding my smocks' proposal. Hang it all, can't you see why British industry is so down-at-heel? It's because of this sort of sluggishness.

Yours, &c
HRH The Prince of Wales

Sir Philip Green
Topshop
Oxford Street
London
England   22 January 2011

Dear Sir Philip

Four days, now. This quite beggars belief! The Minister at the
Department of Trade & Industry will be hearing about this.

Yours, &c
HRH The Prince of Wales

Dealings With International Statesmen

General Idi Amin
c/o Ugandan High Commission
Uganda House
Trafalgar Square
London
England   1 February 1971

Greetings!

I'm writing to you as a representative of Black Africa. I have
frequently met and jostled intimately with your people,
particularly the womenfolk (not specifically Ugandan, but in a
more general sense) and have always found them remarkably
friendly. Cheerful poverty seems to be the order of the day in
your continent – here, we have our televisions, electric stoves
and yet we're so often down in the dumps. Tell me, as a jolly
man yourself, what is the secret that which we sick blighters of
the West have lost? Is it a potion, some proverb? I'd be curious
to know and feel sure I could send you on a Royal gift of sorts
by way of exchange. Do you like teak?

        Yours, in good faith
        HRH The Prince of Wales

Malcolm Fraser
The Prime Minister's Office
Canberra
Australia   12 April 1976

Dear Mr Fraser

I must say, I am most disappointed to be rejected for the job of
Governor-General of Australia. One feels somewhat slapped in
the face. What, may I ask was the problem with my candidacy?
At twenty-eight, am I too old? That strikes me as ridiculous.
It's not as if I don't know the country – I spent some weeks
there in my youth and got to know the 'ordinary' Australian
'chap' quite well, at 'first hand'.

Hang it all, with the greatest of respect, there you are down
there in the bottom right-hand corner of the map! It's not as if
you're at the centre or crux of world affairs. And you know, I
simply wasn't going to sit in a big house on the hill in a plumed
hat doing nothing – I would have got things done. I expect you
need things done, don't you? Well, I would have done them!
On some islands not too far away from you, the natives worship
my father as some sort of stone God. Are you aware of this? I
find that too-large island states can sometimes get above
themselves and lose touch with their original, spiritual
simplicity.

    Yours, in high dudgeon
    HRH The Prince of Wales

Malcolm Fraser
The Prime Minister's Office
Canberra
Australia   17 April 1976

Dear Mr Fraser

Thank you for the response from your office, over which
whomsoever was responsible evidently laboured hard for some
minutes. I should observe that I am referred to as 'Your Royal
Highness', not 'Your Worship' nor, as I am just one line later,
'Your Honour'.

>   Yours, underlined with emphasis
>   HRH The Prince of Wales

Mikhail Gorbachev
c/o The Kremlin
The Union of Soviet Socialist Republics   6 July 1986

Dear Mr Gorbachev

According to our Prime Minister, Mrs Thatcher, you are 'a
man we can do business with'. Between ourselves as gentlemen,
anyone who can do business with *that* lady – who has all the
obduracy of an Oscar Wilde aunt – is a man who can do
business with *anybody*!

Which is why I am writing. As relations between our two
great nations thaw, it seems to me that we have a chance to work
together in a harmonious and co-operative spirit. Let's drop
the pretence, neither you nor Great Britain really want to
perish in a global nuclear annihilation – it's all a bit of bluff.

What we need to do is talk, two eminent men of the world, you and me. Of course, you don't have any English and my Russky is a bit rusty. What's more, having some translator fellow hanging around is no good either — it's like having an inexperienced, over-attentive footman at the dining table, breathing down one's neck. We all know what that's like!

May I, therefore, make a practical suggestion? At an arranged summit meeting I shall have sent for one of my most favoured tomato plants from Highgrove, which is well used to the sound of my voice and in flourishing annually has shown itself to be a most excellent listener. I propose each of us in turn talks to the plant, expressing our mutual goodwill and willingness to move forward. The plant will absorb this goodwill; the tomatoes it will yield, both this year and in the future, will be the fruit of our dialogue, working their way back into nature's system and thereby spreading positive emanations. We could film the thing live for posterity. The plant's name is Emily — named after Emily Bishop, a very famous television character in our country. I have always felt she would be a good listener.

> Attentively, yours
> HRH The Prince of Wales

Mikhail Gorbachev
c/o The Kremlin
The Union of Soviet Socialist Republics   6 July 1986

Dear Mr Gorbachev

I'm afraid the dangers of a translator have been well highlighted in the response from your man. He seems under the impression that we convene to talk at a tomato canning plant! That wasn't what I meant at all. What must you think of me?

I enclose the original letter, with a Russian translation provided by one of my reliable staff of the relevant sentence in the margin, plus an illustration of a plant by oneself to 'ram home' my meaning.

>   Yours, &c
>   HRH The Prince of Wales

The Mayor of (West) Berlin
Berlin
West Germany   12 June 1989

Dear Sir

I recently had cause to pass through your side of the city for a conference on Alternative Chiropody, a subject very close to my heart to say nothing of my toes (forgive my English humour!). Like a great many people, I was saddened to witness the rather depressing spectacle of the Berlin Wall, particularly the graffiti with which it is covered, one of the great blights and curses of the modern age.

May I advance a radical suggestion, which could historically alter Berlin as we stand on the brink of the 1990s? Foliage. Herbaceous coverage. Greenery. Hang it all, the wall can't be knocked down, but at least it needn't be a hideous spectacle of bare, inhuman concrete of the sort that drags down the spirits in every modern city, every day! I suggest a mixture of ivy, creeping plants and so forth, shrubbery covering every last inch of the wall from one end to the next, so that it's not such a 'karbunkel' (ich habe ein bisschen Deutsch).

By 1999, my vision of the Berlin Wall is that it be known as the 'Berlin Hedge'. In time, who knows? The shrubbery might even lead to a greater understanding and harmony between East and Western Berliners and from that, who knows?

Yours, in spiritual assistance!
HRH The Prince of Wales

Nelson Mandela
Praetoria
South Africa
Africa   17 August 1994

Dear Mr Mandela

Congratulations on achieving the office of President with a clear mandate from your people! I have always admired your courage in fighting against the apartheid regime, which I found abhorrent. To me, to discriminate against a man because of the colour of his skin is as ridiculous as being prejudiced because of the shape of his knees.

I was privileged to travel to your country and may I suggest as your first order of business that you do something about the amount of litter in some of the outlying towns. I was driven through one area, which was mile after mile of ghastly mess – randomly strewn corrugated iron, bits of cloth hung over sticks, rusty old stewpots and so forth. It would probably require a squadron of bulldozers to sort it all out and clear it away, but I should get on to it right away, the sooner the better.

Yours, moving forward together
HRH The Prince of Wales

The Norwegian Ambassador
c/o Norwegian Embassy
Belgrave Square
London
England   12 January 1999

Dear Sir

I write to you on a matter of some delicacy. I'm optimistic,
however, at the end of this correspondence our two countries
can continue to move forward together as friends. Allow me to
explain: we were in the drawing room the other evening, the
whole family, when the conversation (which had been rather
slow) turned for some reason towards the subject of Norway.
My father, Prince Philip, stared into the fireplace and his brow
darkened. For some reason, your country's annual gesture of
sending us a Christmas tree for Trafalgar Square in thanks for
the efforts of our armed forces in World War II rather
exercised him.

'Norway!' he spluttered. 'Hauled their scraggy, surrendering
Scandinavian backsides out of the Second World War and what
do they give us in return? A tree, a bloody tree! Not even
decorated, I'll warrant. Well, thank you very much, you
herring-munching suicide cases!'

'Bloody right!' piped up my grandmother, HM Queen
Elizabeth The Queen Mother, who had had, shall we say, a
restful afternoon. 'Quislings!' she yelped.

'Now, now . . . steady on, father,' I interjected at this point.
'The Norwegians, you know, they've made a tremendous and
enriching post-war contribution, with any number of
statesmen, artists, scientists, architects . . . gardeners?'

'Name one!' grunted Father.

And you know what? I couldn't – which rather suspended
the debate. I was wondering, Ambassador, if you could furnish

me with a list of eminent post-war Norwegians that I might reel off the next time this topic comes up? It would help greatly if they were ones I'd already heard of, but had forgotten about to save having to read up. Oh, and no need to include that excitable football commentator – the 'your boys took a hell of a beating' fellow – I don't think he'd cut much ice.

>Internationally yours
>HRH The Prince of Wales

The Norwegian Ambassador
c/o Norwegian Embassy
Belgrave Square
London
England   12 January 1999

Dear Sir

Thank you for the pamphlet prepared by your staff, with its list and potted biographies of eminent modern Norwegians.

I'm afraid, however, that I had heard of none of them. If you will recall, I did specify Norwegians I had heard of. Could you have your people prepare another piece of literature on that basis?

>Yours, &c
>HRH The Prince of Wales

George W. Bush
The White House
Washington
United States of America   20 January 2001

Dear Mr Bush

I am reliably informed by my people that you belong to one of
the five oldest families in the United States and are distantly
related to the English Royal Family, all of which makes your
transformation into a cow-punching, 'good old' Texan country
boy the more impressive.

   I congratulate you on attaining the highest rank your
country allows and am gladdened to hear you talk of
compassionate conservatism. In other words, it's always going
to be the rich man at his castle, the poor man at his gate but for
form's sake, at least have the decency to make a sad face about
it! We had a Prime Minister, Mrs Thatcher, who wasn't always
good at doing this. Mention the poor to her at a function and
she was apt to look away and wrinkle her face, as if having
caught a waft from the drains.

   None of that for you! I hear you reach out to the Hispanics,
to the ethnic communities, and most of all, to the regular,
patriotic 'Joe Six-Pack' in his checked shirt, turning an honest
dollar. I would urge you, Mr Bush, if anything not to lose sight
of the well-to-do, the major wealth creators, the big company
owners or the multi-billionaires. You will protect their
interests too, won't you? They, too, have their part to play in a
harmonious, balanced society as well as everyday working
patriots, who appear to be your natural sort.

           Yours, in hope
           HRH The Prince of Wales

George W. Bush
The White House
Washington
United States of America   20 January 2005

Dear Mr Bush

Well, it seems you have been voted in for a second term. The
Americans must see something in you, I suppose. I'm glad you
heeded my message about not allowing your oft-professed
affinity with 'regular' humble folk to deflect from attending
also to the interests of the well-to-do — you certainly seem to
have done that.

   Did you ever meet President Nixon? I did, in 1969. I would
have supposed you President types were pushed for time, with
fellows in dark glasses moving you along every few minutes, but
at this function — at which he may have been the worse for
wear — he spoke to me for fully an hour and a half about
everything from HM The Queen to Russia, to China, to my
marriage prospects, to being on constant guard against one's
enemies, to the Jewish people — for whom he no more cared
than did my late grandmother. At one point he bade us both
kneel in prayer to 'the one Christian God', after which I had to
help him up — at which point he forgot who I was and mistaking
me for an over-fussy aide, showered me with a stream of
invective. I made my excuses and departed.

   You're a teetotaller, aren't you, Mr Bush? Probably just as
well, taken in the round.

           Yours, &c
           HRH The Prince of Wales

Georg Boomgaarden
German Ambassador to the UK
23 Belgrave Square
London
England   1 August 2005

Dear Ambassador Boomgaarden

It is a pleasure to correspond with you. We're both busy men
and the Germans are a proud people, so I think we can at long
last dispense with referring to the whole World War II
business — we're past that. My father is of another generation
and occasionally apt to remark crisply on the subject but we are
of the younger generation, keen to 'modernise and move
forward together', to use Churchill's phrase.

As you may know, my youngest boy recently attended a fancy
dress party dressed as a Nazi. *Jugend* will be *Jugend*, I suppose, but
he didn't realise the offence caused and I had to deliver him
something of a 'sermon' about stereotypes and so forth. As a
practical example, I had one of my staff send out for a Digital
Versatile Disc (or 'DVD') of a German situation comedy series
(*Rolf! Dein Schwanzstucker*) to scotch the idea Germans have no
sense of humour. Unfortunately, on arrival, it had no subtitles.

I hoped, therefore, that you might come down to
Highgrove — it'd be myself, you and Harry — and we could go
through the DVD, frame by frame, with you translating the
jokes and explaining to us why they are so amusing. I think this
would make for a most stimulating, educating and, above all,
uproarious evening. Now we are at peace, I suppose you have
plenty of time on your hands.

> Yours, in European brotherhood
> HRH The Prince of Wales

Georg Boomgaarden
German Ambassador to the UK
23 Belgrave Square
London
England   4 August 2005

Dear Ambassador Boomgaarden

I am disappointed you are unable to find time in the
foreseeable future to come down to Highgrove and talk Harry
and me through the DVD. I find it hard to believe your diary is
full. What do you do all day? This is important business — I
can't promise the lad won't do something like this again, you
know. Judging by his grandfather, the 'repeat offence' gene is
quite strong in our family.

>   Yours, &c
>   HRH The Prince of Wales

The Spanish Ambassador
c/o The Spanish Embassy
London
England   14 October 2006

Dear Sir

'Hola!' It's my habit, whenever I can find the time, to do
some sort of 'round robin' of the United Kingdom's friendly
near-European neighbours to see how they are 'getting
along' and if there is any role that I, as heir, might play in
helping them move forward. I found myself with a free
morning and after consulting my file, realised it was a while

since I had written to your embassy – some fifteen years, in
fact.

So, how are you getting along? Well, I trust. I have always
taken a great interest in Spain, its people, its customs, its
animals, its trees. Buildings, too – its buildings – marshlands?

Well, the telephone appears to be ringing so I must go and
answer it. It has been a pleasure to correspond. A prompt reply
would be greatly appreciated for my records.

> Yours, er . . . yours
> HRH The Prince of Wales

President Barack Obama
The White House
Washington
USA   1 January 2009

Dear Mr Barack

If that is the term? Dash these formalities! Officially, I'm 'HRH
The Prince of Wales' but you can just call me 'Sir'.
Congratulations on your famous election victory. As a half-
black man, you must feel half-proud for all black people
everywhere, as well as all half-black people. We stayed up and
watched the results come in as a family – certain of whom made
certain remarks which they considered drily humorous
concerning yourself, but I shan't pass those on. After all, we are
not all 'modernists'.

I was especially taken with your catchphrase: 'Yes, We Can!'
Rousing stuff! I was wondering if I might use it myself? Like
you, I have a vision – that a wrecking ball be taken to the
gruesome glass-and-metal monstrosities that disfigure both the

North and South Banks of the River Thames and that they be replaced by thatched cottages to serve as commoners' dwellings. When next waxing this topic at the podium, it'd be nice to be able to throw in the phrase, perhaps adapted a little, to rebuke the naysayers: 'Yes, One Can!' Can one, to lapse into the parlance of your (half) people, get a witness?

> Soulfully, yours
> HRH The Prince of Wales

His Holiness Benedict XVI
c/o The Vatican
Vatican City
Rome
Italy   10 October 2009

Your Holiness

I hope this correspondence finds you well. I extend this letter to you in a warm and ecumenical spirit, although I am most dismayed at the scandals currently enveloping the Catholic Church, what with child abuse and so forth. I know this has caused you great pain and I fully sympathise with you. Because, you see, I myself was abused as a child.

When I say 'abused', it was more in the nature of ragging, really: Gordonstoun. Chinese burns, being forced to run starkers apart from a face flannel from the changing rooms to the dorm after some tittering blighter made off with one's clothes, an initiation ritual involving a jar of salad cream and a mop (which out of respect for Your Holiness I shan't elaborate on further). All character building, or so I was told.

Anyway, I do hope it's of some comfort to know that although we are of different faiths, we are in a strange sense, 'in the same boat'.

> May our God be with us
> HRH The Prince of Wales

PS I hesitate to forward any criticism of Your Holiness but whoever is advising you to smile for the cameras may be mistaken. Without at all meaning to do so, you have a way of 'leering', which is unfortunate in the present climate (one thinks of 'puppies' or 'sweets'). I say this with immense respect.

The French Ambassador
c/o The French Embassy
Knightsbridge
London
England   12 March 2010

Monsieur

Bonjour!
Si vous êtes content, je voudrais ecrire ce lettre en Français — j'ai un peu de Français mais seulement un peu, vous savez. Pour pratiquer, je n'emploi pas un dictionaire. Pardonnez les erreurs!
   Je pense que nos nations ont beaucoup en commone — ('common'? *Comment dit-on?*) Actually, on second thoughts, probably just as well for me to abandon this particular experiment — I might goof badly and create a diplomatic incident! There was talk of me becoming Ambassador to France, back in 1979; what they'd nowadays call 'work experience', I suppose. Lord Carrington, who was one of Mrs Thatcher's men, described the idea as

'crazy' and I suppose he had a point. Clearly, I was cut out for bigger things and would probably have been by way of being 'overqualified' for the job, certainly in terms of eminence.

That said maybe there is merit in the suggestion. I was wondering, should an opening arise, if my youngest son Harry might be put up for French Ambassador? He's the ginger one, in case you need a prompt. Granted there was that business a while back in which he dressed up in full Nazi regalia for some fancy-dress party and the press got wind of it and kicked off a stink. Some might say that disqualifies him for the job, especially with the French having spent most of World War II with the Nazi jackboot at their neck following the Maginot bungle and sensibilities could be ruffled by his appointment. But let's look at this from the other side. For me, this is precisely why such a job would be good for the lad! It'd help teach him something of the nuances of international diplomacy, the delicacy of national feelings and give him a bit of history and geography. A few years as French Ambassador and I'd be willing to 'bet' the chances of him turning up to some function, clicking his heels as he's announced at the door and goose-stepping in dressed as Josef Goebbels would be pretty much negligible.

Constructively, yours
HRH The Prince of Wales

The French Ambassador
c/o The French Embassy
Knightsbridge
London
England   12 March 2010

Monsieur

In answer to your letter, yes, I was perfectly serious, *absolument
serieux*! Quelle question étrange, mon bon homme!

  Yours, &c
  HRH The Prince of Wales

Beyond the Hurly-Burly of the Industrial Era: Spirituality and the New Age

The Most Revd the Archbishop of Canterbury
Lambeth Palace
London
England   16 July 1957

Dear Archbishop

I'm very worried about God and thought that I should write to
you about it. After all, you're awfully closer to our Lord and
probably talk to Him all day, not just before bedtime, like I do.

Last year, Mummy took me to one side and told me there
was no Father Christmas. The year before, she informed me
there was no such thing as the Easter Bunny. And the year
before that, she said there was no such thing as the Tooth Fairy.
So, this year, I'm expecting her to tell me there's no such thing
as God, and I want to be ready this time and not burst into
tears as I have in the past.

Is there really no God, then? And if not, why do you dress
up like that? Is it just pretend, like Santa's elves? I suppose
you're like God's elf, really, helping Him out down here,
keeping everything nice and tidy for when He comes next. Or is
Mummy going to wait till I'm a teenager before she tells me
there's no God? Or does everyone know there's no God except
you because your mummy didn't tell you? In that case . . . oops,
sorry!

　　　　Yours, trying to be brave
　　　　HRH The Prince of Wales

The Most Revd the Archbishop of Canterbury
Lambeth Palace
London
England   7 April 1958

Dear Archbishop

Guess what? Yesterday, I was just talking, at the table, when
Anne turned to me and for no reason said, 'You really are the
most boring, boring, boring, BORING boy ever!'

Will God send her to hell for committing the sin of
rudeness? I do wish he wouldn't, because even though she's just
a smelly old girl, I would miss her in heaven. Perhaps God
could send one of her horses to hell instead and make her
watch as he does this? Because that would REALLY make her
cry! Or he could dangle the horse just above hell and pretend
he was about to drop it in, but not do it at the last minute. Yes,
that would be best because then the horse wouldn't have to be
burnt, just be a bit scared, but Anne would still cry – which
serves her right for being rude!

   Yours, in mercy
   HRH The Prince of Wales

The Prince Charles Letters

The Most Revd the Archbishop of Canterbury
Lambeth Palace
London
England   12 June 1958

Dear Archbishop

My Uncle Dickie says that one day I will have to pick myself a
wife. I hope I will choose wisely. Have you ever heard the tale of
the Frog and the Princess, Archbishop? It's about a Princess
who kisses a frog and the frog turns into a Prince and the
Prince becomes a King, and then they live happily ever after. I
know that sort of thing doesn't happen in 'real life' but it gives
me a great idea, which I think I will try out when I'm old and
need to look for a wife.

What we could do, OK, is have all the women who want to
be Queen sit in a waiting room, all six or seven of them. Then,
through a secret door, one of the footmen could pass through
about twelve or thirteen frogs from a box into the room, all
hopping about the place and going, 'Ribbit! Ribbit!' All the
women who start screaming and jumping on to their chairs,
they'd be told to go home and come back another time. But the
one who picked up a frog and kissed it, she'd be Queen,
because that would be kind to the frog and just what a Queen
would do. And then I'd appear from another door and say,
'Congratulations! We're getting married.' And we'd get
married, and go shooting and live happily ever after.

Cheerfully, yours
HRH The Prince of Wales

The Most Revd the Archbishop of Canterbury
Lambeth Palace
London
England   14 December 1958

Dear Archbishop

I heard a hymn — a carol, I think, although it might just have
been a Christmas song — all about God and how he watches you
at all times, even when you're sleeping, to check you're not
doing anything wrong. Does he really? I've hardly been able to
go to the bathroom all week because I get embarrassed if I think
someone's watching me and then I can't go. Then I got tummy-
ache and had to go and see Nurse, and when I told her about it
all the other boys in the sickbay laughed and I went bright red.
     The next time you talk to God, could you ask him to look
the other way while I'm on the loo? I promise him I'm not
doing anything bad, just number ones or number twos. I'd ask
him myself, but I'm too shy.

          Yours, urgently
          HRH The Prince of Wales

The Most Revd the Archbishop of Canterbury
Lambeth Palace
London
England   1 January 1960

Dear Archbishop

In our Divinity class yesterday, our teacher was talking about the reasons why God exists and he said that the best reason of all was 'Design'. That means you can tell the Universe was made by a God because when you look at things like a snail or a worm, you can tell they've been crafted by hand. The stars are like that, too.

Except when I look at the sky through my telescope, it doesn't really seem like it's been designed, it looks like there was a big bang and everything went BOOOOSSSSSSSSSHHHHH! and bits of rock were scattered far and wide.

But suppose God did design the Universe, wouldn't He have signed it? Suppose you got a really, really powerful telescope and pointed it to the skies in the direction of the bottom right-hand corner of outer space and there was a group of stars all clustered together and arranged into the letters, 'Made by God'. That's what I'd have done, if I'd been God and made all creation. Have you got Astronomers you could ask to look and see if it's there, because then we'd really know?

Yours, as every week
HRH The Prince of Wales

The Sikh Community Leader
Hounslow
London
England   8 July 1977

Dear Sir

Before I begin, I must first welcome your community to this
country with open arms. With your warrior spirit, pride and
determination to succeed, I feel that you have the makings of
great Britons.

However, already I note that we have found ourselves at a
quandary, with UK law requiring motorcyclists to wear crash
helmets but your people objecting because this prevents them
from wearing the sacred turban. It is terrible to think that as a
result of this we may never on these shores see a Sikh Barry
Sheen – something must be done, though currently I am not
sure what.

I am, though, impressed by the idea of you having a
Community Leader. In our country, it is the custom to have
elected political officials. Some say this is a more sophisticated
way of doing things, but I myself sometimes wonder if we have
lost a certain wisdom in this regard that you Sikhs have
maintained.

> Yours, most graciously
> HRH The Prince of Wales

Drivers Jonas
Planning Consultants   16 September 1988

Dear Sirs

Recently, I've been rather 'goaded' by Mr Richard Rogers in
particular into putting my money where my mouth is and
establishing a practical architectural example of the way I feel
Britons would live in harmony with nature, their own souls and
the Monarchy.

What I propose is this – a model village near Dorchester, where
I have land. It could shine like a candle as an example as to other
villages, towns – even city planners. Its dwellings would be modest,
as befits the character of the British subject. They would reflect the
characteristics key to my vision of Britain – scale, harmony,
hierarchy, locality, tone, spirit, elevation, humility, conservation,
thrift, proportion, good grammar, diffidence, obedience (to
nature, our benefactor or to benefactors in general).

As to the village's name, I have as yet dashed out a few
preliminary thoughts – Charlesville? Charlie-on-Sea? Littler
London? Princonia? But an idea of its character is fermenting
in my imagination. Here is a village redolent of a merrier
England, of maypole dances, russets and fayres, Shire horses,
scythes, in which no subject feels the need at any time from
cradle to grave to move more than six to ten yards from their
dwelling place. Everything is at hand, all humble needs catered
for – this is how we would live. Or *they*, I should say, for my
duties would keep me at Highgrove and the Palace.

And what name would we give to those who would live in
these communities, which will surely become 'all the rage' in
the 1990s? Peasants? Perhaps unwise – how about 'Pleasants'?

Rustically, yours
HRH The Prince of Wales

The Plant Kingdom   6 April 1989

To Whom It May Concern

This letter is not intended for public circulation of any sort — it may be seized on and misunderstood. I have kept a copy for my files but the original I have buried in my garden as a symbolic gesture of delivery although perhaps in some sort of rhizome-type underground movement, its message might in ways as yet unknown to man spread and be transmitted from plant to plant.

In some quarters I am ridiculed among man for talking to plants but the truth is, I have only been lucky enough to talk to a tiny number of you. This letter is intended as a long overdue salute. As plants, you perform a vital function: you sustain the life we enjoy on this earth. I'm not entirely certain of the science but essentially it's to do with carbon and oxygen.

Our science fiction writers have sometimes presented the notion of plants taking over the planet as a 'nightmare scenario' and yet would you make such a poor fist of running things, I often wonder. Then again, you are a gentle species group, not given to domination or tyranny. Asking only for water and the occasional kind word, you do not cavil or make fun of a man's ears, abandon your roots or answer back. The antidote to cement and concrete, you are in total and quiet accordance with nature. Not for nothing do I often wish I were destined not to reign over men, but to reign over plants —you're a lot less bother.

> Yours, the Defender of all Species
> HRH The Prince of Wales

To: Appointed Alien Leader   18 January 1999

Dear ?

This letter is to be read out in the event of an extraterrestrial invasion of Great Britain, being the authentic words, directly committed to stationery paper, of His Royal Highness Prince Charles, The Prince of Wales, KG KT GCB OM AK QSO CD SOM GCL PC AdC(P) FRS, Defender of Many Faiths. It may seem unlikely aliens will ever arrive here, but then whoever imagined the Internet or a telephone you could play the latest popular tunes on? One never knows, so one must anticipate all eventualities.

First of all, assuming your intentions are as friendly as those of our own, seafaring English ancestors who sought out new lands and opportunities, I welcome you. I am sure we have a good deal to learn from each other. It is your custom, I understand, to address those you visit on a new planet with the words, 'Take me to your leader!' (I once saw a jolly funny cartoon in *The Hotspur* of a little green, slitty-eyed fellow with wires coming out of his head standing next to a fire hydrant and saying to it, 'Take me to your leader!' That's something you'll soon discover about us British — our sense of humour. But I digress.)

The thing is, in this country the leader isn't actually the King, which I might well be by the time you arrive, but whoever lives at a place called 10 Downing Street (it's the way we do things). However, if you don't like our way of doing things and would rather talk to me, that can most certainly be arranged. If you're part of a successful invasion force, you'd doubtless be 'calling the shots'.

> Yours, with greetings and salutations
> HRH The Prince of Wales

PS Do you have a faith? If so, allow me to defend it.

Alan Milburn (Minister for Health)
House of Commons
London
England   16 May 2003

Dear Mr Milburn

Every year, we're losing thousands of man-hours to illness. It's
time to face facts: modern medicine simply isn't working. We
need alternative treatments — herbal, shiatsu, all this wonderful
ancient medical wisdom we have sloshing about — well, not the
ancient wisdom of dentistry, of course, which essentially
consisted of a fellow hacking at another fellow's rotten tooth
with a piece of flint while two other fellows held him down —
but a lot of the other sorts, and especially homeopathy.

Many people think of homeopathy as some sort of ill-
founded quackery conceived by a crackpot. In fact, it's anything
but this: it was discovered by a Mr Samuel Hahnemann, back in
1796. Yes, a German, I know — but hear me out. Mr
Hahnemann thought long and hard and discovered the best way
to cure an ailment was to treat 'like with like', using an element
of what caused the ailment in the first place, diluting it and
rapping the container of the solution precisely twelve times
against a leather-bound book in order to release its dynamic
forces. Must be a *leather*-bound book, mind — none of your
modern paperbacks or it won't work. And twelve times, not
eleven, not thirteen: twelve. A lot of people think I'm making
this up, but I'm not.

Now, here's the thing: water has a memory. We must accept
that. It further follows the more you dilute the homeopathic
solution — thousands upon thousands of times — the stronger
the memory will get. Well, it would, wouldn't it? Leap with me,
Minister! I recommended a homeopathic treatment to my PA
(with extract from rose hip, one of nature's little givers) when

233

she complained of a slight migraine and after several treatments she told me that yes, perhaps she was feeling a little better, or at least possibly so. I'd take that ringing personal endorsement from a trusted employee over a hundred of your so-called 'evidence-based studies'.

> Yours, in faith and healing
> HRH The Prince of Wales

Alan Milburn (Minister for Health)
House of Commons
London
England   17 May 2003

Dear Mr Milburn

Further to our correspondence regarding homeopathy, a treatment was recently brought to my attention. It is promoted as a cure for a range of ailments, from rheumatism to high fever. To prepare it, you will need a large copper pan (it must be copper, mind – otherwise the treatment will not work!). Into this dice precisely six grams of fresh parsley, three grams of autumn crocus, then add a dozen milligrams of elderflower extract and – here is the remarkable part – a pint and a half of your own urine. Heat and mix, and then, once it has cooled, tap the pan and its contents nine times on your cranium while incanting the word 'Chumbawamba!' over and over. Then consume.

I must admit that I was uncertain of its benefits, though it did appear to work quite effectively as a laxative. On that basis, I agreed to take part in a short promotional video demonstrating the preparation and ingestion of the solution. However, it then emerged that the whole treatment was a 'prank' dreamt up by a medical student. Fortunately, news of my involvement was suppressed – not a word about this to anyone, Minister.

This is a cautionary tale. We must beware of bogus treatments, ridiculous placebos that have no effect except in the imagination of pitiful fools, as distinguished from authentic, proven treatments like homeopathy.

> Yours, in vigilance
> HRH The Prince of Wales

To: Mankind   8 July 2005

This is perhaps the most presumptuous, but perhaps also the most momentous letter I have written in the entire history of my correspondence. But hang it all, it's one thing addressing this or that man – or, indeed, woman or boy! When does one ever address Mankind, that transcendent human entity to which we all belong? And that is what I propose to do here.

Mankind, I have been worried about you for a long time now. In body, you seem fit enough, though our forefathers might be struck by our increased circumferences, a world in which a Harry Secombe-type physique no longer seems quite out of the ordinary, to be singled out for decades of comic treatment. Your soul, however, is shrivelled as an old, dried-out bladder. What is to be done? Fresh air, I suppose; a reconnection with soil and the natural rhythms of nature. Perhaps. For you to adopt the ways of the Kalahari Bushman, with an ear to the ground and the decrees of the true earth long suppressed by the cacophony of heavy machinery and the clever, but misguided diktats of the intellect.

Yes, that's it! Live the lives of Bushmen. Pots, grubs, spears, and so forth . . . Cast aside your washing machines and music decks. That, ultimately, should be your goal. Make that your aim, mankind, all of you, in time! How I envy the Africans in particular, who are closer to this ideal than any of us. I shall observe your progress from Highgrove with great interest and frequent encouragement.

Yours, in solidarity
HRH The Prince of Wales

To: The IOP (Institute of Physics)
76–78 Portland Place
London
England   16 April 2007

Gentlemen (and ladies, should that be appropriate)

For centuries, physicists have striven to grasp that holiest of grails, one which would satisfy all our energy needs in a stroke – the perpetual motion machine. And now, working in my potting shed with the assistance of selected members of staff, I can announce that I feel sure I'm on the cusp of what would be the greatest scientific discovery of the age.

I have enclosed a diagram of the device: it consists of a ping-pong ball proceeding down a descending arrangement of slides, finally returning to a point directly below where it began its journey. But how to return it to that point? I suggest a column of water in a glass tube, which the ball enters before floating up to the top, thereby placing it in a position to resume its circuit. Perpetual motion!

There are just two snags – how to get the ball to enter the column of water, and once it's floated to the top, impelling it to start sliding down the slide again. At the moment, it requires a couple of nudges for the perpetual circuit to work. It stymies me, but hang it all, gentlemen, that's how close we are – just nudges away from freedom from our dependence on fossil fuels, oil and nuclear energy! I've practically done all the work and I leave it for you boffins to simply provide the final push over the 'top'. These are exciting times, are they not?

> Yours, in soaring optimism
> HRH The Prince of Wales

Professor Brian Cox
University of Manchester
Manchester
England   18 January 2011

Dear Professor Cox

I've been greatly enjoying your series on the BBC and admire the way you bring science into the home of the everyday 'fellow'. I don't know if you're the right person to whom to address this brainwave I've had, but I suppose you'd be kind enough to pass it on if it's not your 'department' because that's literally what I'm talking about – brainwaves.

I don't know about you, but I spend a lot of time simply thinking and I hate to think it's just being frittered away. I'm sure I'm not the only one who thinks a lot – thousands, millions of us do. Is there not a way of harnessing all that mental energy and putting it to some positive, practical use? I was thinking of some sort of hat lined with tin foil, remotely connected to a small grid. I'm sure my cogitating on a single afternoon would be enough to power a domestic vacuum cleaner for at least half an hour's 'hoovering'. We can put a man on the moon, surely we can place a tin-lined hat on his head? You manufacture it using your 'know-how', Professor Cox, and I'll wear it.

> Yours, in the hope of things getting better
> HRH The Prince of Wales

John Cook
Chairman
British Homeopathic Association
Hahnemann House
29 Park Street West
Luton
England   10 February 2011

Dear Mr Cook

Congratulations! As people slowly come to realise the real answer to what ails us lies beyond science, medicine and knowledge, homeopathy is making headway into the NHS and becoming increasingly accessible to all. On Charing Cross Road, where once were bookshops, are now outlets offering New Age remedies, potions and crystals – this is progress.

With this boom, however, lies a danger: you must have read recently of the attempted suicide of the daughter of pop singer Billy Joel, who took an overdose of homeopathic medicine. Somehow she survived, but we must be alert to the dangers of our young people abusing homeopathic products, either for 'kicks' or some self-destructive purpose.

To avert this peril, I would be glad to present a Public Information film, warning young people against homeopathy misuse. To make the piece more harrowing, it would help if you could furnish me with case studies — there must be hundreds of them — of people who have made themselves ill (or even died) through overdosing on homeopathic pills.

> Yours, with great urgency
> HRH The Prince of Wales

John Cook
Chairman
British Homeopathic Association
Hahnemann House
29 Park Street West
Luton
England   16 February 2011

Dear Mr Cook

According to my records, I have yet to receive a response concerning my public information initiative to combat the widespread phenomenon of homeopathic overdose. I assume you must have entire cabinets dedicated to files of recorded cases. It might be that you consider the photographic evidence of victims, convulsed by the excess of active ingredients in the average homeopathic pill, to be too grisly for Royal eyes to behold but don't spare me, I am not squeamish! On the other hand, please don't 'swamp' me. Just send me a dozen or so of the most really, really appalling cases.

> Yours &c
> HRH The Prince of Wales

John Cook
Chairman
British Homeopathic Association
Hahnemann House
29 Park Street West
Luton
England   22 February 2011

Dear Mr Cook

I just had a member of my staff call your offices concerning the
photos I requested, only to be informed there are no recorded
cases whatsoever of death by homeopathic overdose. Either this
was due to a faulty telephone line, or it strikes me we have been
astoundingly lucky so far. Perhaps a Guiding Hand of some sort
has averted the worst?

Even so, we must not be complacent. May I suggest we use
'human guinea pigs' on which to test the effects of homeopathic
medicine taken to excess? In line with American practice,
perhaps we could take some of Britain's most hardened
criminals, the ones serving life imprisonment, and give them
the choice between serving out their sentences in full or being
set free, if they agree to be experimented on with excess doses of
homeopathic remedies, with the lethal risk that entails. About
eighty or ninety such men would give a broad sample base, I'd
suggest. Shall I inform the Home Secretary or shall you?

    Yours &c
    HRH The Prince of Wales

God
Heaven
Within and Without Us   12 June 2011

Well, God (or Jahweh or Allah, or however you prefer
to be addressed)

I trust You don't mind my corresponding with You like this. A
bit silly, You might think, but although You know all things and
know what I'm about to write, I'm going to write it anyway. You
see, I find that I can best gather and arrange my thoughts set
out in the epistolary form – I expect Your St Peter and Paul felt
the same way. I've tried praying but as well as hurting the knees
like the dickens, I find I get a bit tongue-tied. I don't really
know what to say to You.

Plus, and I don't mean this as any sort of carping criticism,
when I have prayed the rate of return hasn't been all that I
might have desired. You may well remember, I expect You do,
that I prayed very hard to You in my Gordonstoun days – some
of them were a bit silly, like the plague of boils I requested to be
visited on Tubby Southbridge, the boy who led the delegation
that forced me to drink the contents of my own inkwell through
a stripy straw. I can understand Your vetoing that one. But
then, on those long, sleepless, lonely nights, praying that
Mummy and Daddy would the next morning come bowling up
in the big car and whisk me away from that ghastly, fiend-filled
Caledonian chamber of sado-masochistic misery, back to tea
and hearth and Nanny – did You hear me, I wondered? I have
to believe You did.

All water under the bridge, I suppose. Anyway, the reason
I'm writing is this. It used to be commonly believed that the
Monarch of England was divinely appointed. Not so widespread
nowadays, that idea, but in the spirit of Pascal, I always think it's
worth hedging one's bets. So, given you're divine and I'm next

in line to be appointed, I was wondering – suppose You were to send me a sign, via Nature, giving me either the thumbs-up or thumbs-down as regards my future prospects on the throne?

What I have in mind, Sir, is this. Among my most favoured hounds is my basset Woodrow, who out of affection and respect for his age, I allow to sleep in front of the fireplace in my study. Every afternoon, when I come in to attend to my correspondence, he's in the habit of sitting up and barking enthusiastically at me. There follows a bit of give and take before the both of us settle down again: myself to my letters, Woodrow to his slumber.

What I propose is that tomorrow afternoon, in the midst of our give and take, I ask Woodrow the direct question: 'Will I be King?' At this point, Almighty God, I invite You to use him as a vessel through which to express Your will: either have him bark the word 'Yes!' or, should You will it, 'No!' For me, that would settle the matter once and for all, though I am sufficiently sceptical about both the Gentlemen of the Press, to say nothing of certain members of my own family, to suspect my explanation of Woodrow's declaration would not settle the matter for them. Let us therefore keep this between ourselves.

As for this correspondence, I shan't be so daft as to send it out via Royal Mail. I propose, with respect, to throw it on the fireplace in that it may be reduced to ashes and send smoke ascending up the chimney – and symbolically, up into the skies and Heavenward. Assuming You exist (and I believe You do), would You look out for something like this or have one of Your angels keep watch for it? These are deep theological waters.

Most respectfully yours
HRH The Prince of Wales

To God
Heaven
Within and Without Us   13 June 2011

I thought I'd send You a follow-up letter. I listened most
anxiously to each of Woodrow's barks this afternoon. Mostly it
was his usual, common or garden 'woof', but he did at one
point yelp something out of the ordinary. I took the precaution
of 'tape recording' proceedings and playing it back, it sounds
like he was saying, 'Trout!'

Trout? Is there some sort of symbolism, fish-related
perhaps, which I should divine in this? After all, one thinks
of Jesus and His Disciples as 'Fishers of Men'. Perhaps if you
could have Woodrow bark, either in the affirmative or negative,
the same time tomorrow afternoon then I would have
something to reflect deeply upon.

　　　　　Yours &c
　　　　　HRH The Prince of Wales